D1560158

WF Massey

Makers
of the
Modern
World

WF Massey
New Zealand
James Watson

HH
HAUS HISTORIES

First published in Great Britain in 2010 by
Haus Publishing Ltd
70 Cadogan Place
London SW1X 9AH
www.hauspublishing.com

A CIP catalogue record for this book
is available from the British Library

ISBN 978-1-905791-83-5

Series design by Susan Buchanan
Typeset in Sabon by MacGuru Ltd
Printed in Dubai by Oriental Press

Contents

Introduction

United States President Woodrow Wilson was very annoyed. Only that morning an account of discussions at the highest level during the Peace Conference had appeared in a Parisian newspaper, and some of those now in the same room with him were suspected of leaking the information. Someone was taking the President's principle of 'open covenants openly arrived at' much too far. Right now William Massey, the Prime Minister of New Zealand, was speaking, arguing that his country should be given a *fairly clear and definite statement* that it would receive a mandate over Western Samoa and not have to wait until Wilson's brainchild, the League of Nations, was in operation. A large man, with blue eyes, white moustache, a balding head and a ruddy complexion, Massey spoke with traces of the Ulster accent that some of the President's ancestors had used. Wilson was well aware that this farmer from the antipodes was incapable of understanding that the rule of law, operating through the League and backed by the force of international public opinion, would soon make armaments and concerns about 'the balance of power' redundant. He and that insufferable Welshman beside him, William Hughes, Prime Minister of Australia, continued to maintain that their countries needed to control the German colonies on their northern approaches for security reasons.

Suddenly the President had had enough. He demanded to know whether New Zealand and Australia were presenting an ultimatum to the Conference, threatening not to sign the treaty it was drawing up if they were not assured in advance of the mandates over the German colonies they had occupied. Massey was taken aback and denied he was doing this, *but he thought he had made himself perfectly clear*. Thereupon Hughes, fiddling with his primitive hearing aid, deployed an American expression common enough in Australia: 'That's about the size of it, Mr President.' Massey made some sound that David Lloyd George, the British Prime Minister, took to be a grunt of agreement. For a moment it seemed as if Wilson's carefully constructed vision might have to face reality. Would American marines storm ashore in Western Samoa and New Guinea to evict the forces of New Zealand and Australia? Would the rest of the British Empire stand aside while their kith and kin, who had fought beside them on the barren hillsides and parched deserts of the Middle East and the muddy swamps of the Western Front, were subdued? A conciliatory speech from Louis Botha, the Boer commando who had become Prime Minister of South Africa, calmed the atmosphere, and it was followed by reassurances from Massey himself. He declared he was prepared to take personal responsibility for his decision, without referring it back to the New Zealand Parliament. A communiqué was issued, noting that a satisfactory provisional arrangement had been reached. Thus ended what Lloyd George considered 'the only unpleasant episode of the whole Congress'.[1]

Many New Zealanders anticipated great things from the Paris Peace Conference. In New Zealand, as in so many other countries, the experience of a war of unprecedented destructiveness and the hopes propagated by President Wilson led to expectations that the world was about to be transformed. The forthcoming conference was variously described as the 'most momentous conclave in history',[2] 'the most momentous gathering in the political annals of mankind',[3] and 'without parallel in history'.[4] Newspapers followed the progress of negotiations between the victors closely, and many printed the full text of the treaty presented to the Germans. Much less attention was paid to the preparation of the treaties delivered to Austria, Hungary, Bulgaria or Turkey. Indeed, only the latter was regarded as of direct relevance to New Zealand.

As a relatively small power, New Zealand understandably does not loom large in standard accounts of the Paris Peace Conference. However, it does receive some generally unflattering coverage in Margaret MacMillan's *Peacemakers*. Its Prime Minister is described by a Canadian at the Conference as being 'as thick headed and John Bullish as his appearance would lead one to expect'.[5] In accordance with this description, William Massey 'grunts' agreement with Australia's Billy Hughes, opposing President Woodrow Wilson's proposal that the allocation of mandates should be left to the League of Nations.[6] Yet this overlooks the New Zealand Prime Minister's acceptance a few moments later of a compromise that undermined his Australian counterpart. MacMillan mistakenly mocks Massey's statement that Western Samoa was occupied at *great risk* to New Zealand troops.[7] She also leaves open the possibility that Massey may have known that the Western Samoans were opposed to New Zealand rule but stated the opposite to the Supreme Council. The 'squabble' over Nauru with Australia is noted, but not that the outcome was the one for which Massey had worked.[8]

On the Japanese proposal for a racial equality clause to be
included in the Covenant of the League of Nations, 'Massey
of New Zealand followed in Hughes' wake'.[9] Again this
ignores Massey's efforts to find a compromise, efforts that
would probably not have gone down very well back in New
Zealand. MacMillan's account does not do justice to William
Massey or to his contribution to the Conference.[10]

In addition to Massey, New Zealand was represented at the
Conference by Sir Joseph Ward, a previous Prime Minister
and leader of the Liberal Party, which was in the wartime coalition with Massey's Reform Party. Despite his pretensions to
what amounted to equal status, Sir Joseph played a comparatively minor role in Paris. Even his biographer devotes less
than a page to the Conference, most of that not even about
Ward himself.[11] In line with his position as New Zealand Minister of Finance and reputation as a 'financial wizard', Ward
took most interest in how, and the extent to which, Germany
could be brought to pay much of the cost of the war. His
advice to Lloyd George on such matters appears to have been
ignored. It was Massey who spoke for New Zealand.

In 1961, W J Gardner, a historian who was considering
the production of a biography of William Ferguson Massey,
noted that the 'process of biographical revision has been
described as "bunk, debunk and rebunk"'.[12] His own contributions to the process, a slim volume directed at secondary
school students of history and some elegantly written articles, provide a balanced assessment that cannot really be said
to fit in any of those categories.[13] However, there was at least
one hagiography published shortly after Massey's death[14],
and a frankly celebratory work shortly before it.[15] In most
Labour households he had always been regarded as a Prime
Minister set on crushing trade unions and, more generally,

denying the rights of working people. The phrase deployed at the time of the 1913 General Strike for the mounted special police, 'Massey's Cossacks', lived on in popular memory as surely as the term 'Red Fed' for the members of the 'Red' Federation of Labour who backed the strike (and by extension, for any left-wing radical).

More recently, some might argue, the third of the stages outlined by Gardner has been reached. In the mid-1980s Miles Fairburn portrayed Massey as a politician who understood the desire of so much of the New Zealand working class to own their own homes and who appreciated that state assistance to fulfil that desire could be a potent political weapon against his Labour opponents in particular. Far from presenting Massey as an extremist, Fairburn saw him as a bulwark against both the extremists of the Protestant Political Association and those of the labour movement. In 2006 a conference at Massey University, which is named after the Prime Minister, brought together a number of historians who looked at various aspects of Massey's career – almost without exception in a more positive light than had been typical of previous historiography.

This book attempts to give Massey his due, and to examine in particular his role at the Paris Peace Conference and the legacy of the settlements on the country and his later career. Like the other books in this series, this volume begins with a history of the land represented at the Paris Conference and a biography of its representative. Part I is rounded off by a description of how the First World War affected New Zealand and the contributions that the country and its Prime Minister made to the Allied war effort. Part II focuses on the Conference itself, initially setting out New Zealand's interests as interpreted by Massey and his colleagues. It then examines

Massey's performance and mixed success in advancing those interests, before looking at his own and other New Zealanders' reactions to the Treaty of Versailles. Part III looks at the aftermath of the Conference, tracing general developments, both internationally and within New Zealand, that were on the whole rather disappointing to Massey. Finally, the long-term legacy of the Conference for New Zealand is analysed.

William Massey from a portrait by Sir William Orpen

I

The Life and the Land

1
New Zealand to 1914

An emphasis on the youthfulness of New Zealand was a major part of the rhetoric used not only by William Massey and his fellow politicians, but also by the wider settler population of the country in the late 19th and early 20th centuries. They were generally thinking of the relative newness of European settlement, most of it having occurred within the span of one lifetime, and the relative lack of development of its resources. However, New Zealand had also been the last major landmass to be settled by human beings, with Polynesian voyagers probably making landfall around seven hundred years ago. Thereafter a distinctive Maori culture developed, adapted to a generally much cooler climate than that of Polynesia, but also to an archipelago with much greater land and freshwater resources.

Maori-European contact

The earliest known contact between Maori and Europeans occurred in 1642. Two ships of the Dutch East India Company, commanded by Abel Tasman, came upon the western coast of the South Island ('a land uplifted high') when sailing eastwards from Australia. They encountered Maori in what is now Golden Bay. A clash ensued, possibly because the sounding of trumpets by the Dutchmen in reply to similar sounds was taken as a challenge. Four sailors were killed.

Although Tasman's discovery was relatively well known in Europe, no further visit by Europeans seems to have occurred until that of the British ship *Endeavour* in 1769, commanded by Captain James Cook. This was an explicitly scientific expedition, tasked with, amongst other things, observing the transit of the planet Venus across the face of the sun, visible only from a limited area of the South Pacific. A skilled map-maker, Cook charted most of the coastline of New Zealand during the *Endeavour*'s circumnavigation. A French expedition under Jean de Surville was in New Zealand waters at the same time as Cook, who returned in 1773 and 1777.

More substantial European contact with New Zealand and Maori occurred largely as a result of the establishment of the British penal colony in New South Wales in 1788. That colony served as a forward base and to some extent as a market for the exploitation of New Zealand's resources, as well as supplying some runaway convicts as settlers. Parties were landed on the New Zealand coast to hunt seals for their pelts, while the tall trees of the New Zealand rainforest, most famously the *kauri*, attracted interest as a source for naval masts and spars. Likewise, the discovery that Maori could make excellent rope from the fibres of the New Zealand flax (*phormium tenax*) provided another product widely used by shipping. Above all, however, it was the opportunity to hunt whales around New Zealand and to use it as a base and provisioning stop that drew large numbers of ships to its shores from a wide range of countries, not least from the

New England region of the United States. Kororareka in the Bay of Islands, in the far north-east of the North Island, became a major focus for stopovers by whaling ships. Given that some of their prey, most notably the particularly valuable Right Whale, migrated along the New Zealand coast, several stations were also established to hunt from the shore and to draw the carcasses to land for processing. The Europeans manning those stations frequently set up households and raised children with Maori wives.

Maori developed a keen interest in the goods that Europeans brought to trade for provisions, naval supplies, labour and sex. Iron and steel implements rapidly replaced those of stone, while flour, sugar, tobacco and to some extent alcohol became popular. Above all, however, firearms were sought as a means of settling both recent and longstanding grievances against other tribes, of gaining *mana* in victory and of capturing slaves and other booty. Those tribes in areas of greatest European contact were able to secure greater quantities of muskets and steel weaponry to use against their neighbours. Other introductions, such as the potato and, on occasion, sailing ships, assisted the better-equipped tribes to launch and sustain raids over long distances. Nga Puhi from the Bay of Islands area initiated this process with devastating attacks along the east coast of the North Island. Waikato tribes attacked down the western side of the island into Taranaki. Displaced tribes from the Waikato coast (Ngati Toa) and Taranaki (principally Te Atiawa) migrated south under the leadership of the Ngati Toa chief Te Rauparaha, wreaking havoc in their path. They established themselves on Kapiti Island, the adjacent coastline and the Cook Strait area, where the presence of several whaling enterprises afforded good contact with European trade and access to firearms. Te

Rauparaha launched raids down into the South Island. Even the Moriori, isolated for many generations on the Chatham Islands and unaccustomed to warfare, succumbed to invaders from distant Taranaki. The 'musket wars', combined with mortality from introduced diseases, led to a marked decline in Maori population.

New South Wales provided the base for another early wave of European arrivals – the missionaries. Initial interest came from the Reverend Samuel Marsden, a Yorkshire man who had established himself as a landowner and prominent Church of England clergyman in the Sydney area, where he had encountered Maori working on ships. In 1814 he sailed to the Bay of Islands and founded a station for the Church Missionary Society (CMS). The CMS remained the strongest supporter of missionary work in New Zealand, but was soon obliged to share the field with Methodists and later with Catholics. Although initially little progress was made in converting Maori, the missionaries developed a strong concern that unscrupulous Europeans were debauching what they generally saw as a noble race. They were also horrified at the massacres and material destruction of the musket wars. Following widespread Maori conversions in the 1830s, the CMS in particular came to adopt a role as protector of the indigenous people against further European exploitation.

European settlement

The threat of such exploitation loomed large in the late 1830s as Edward Gibbon Wakefield, economist and promoter of colonisation schemes, floated the New Zealand Company in Britain to purchase land in New Zealand and sell it to would-be colonists. Such sales would be at a price 'sufficient' to pay for the establishment of civilised institutions, to assist the immigration of labourers to work in the new colonies, to prevent the development of the uncultured 'squattocracy' of Australia or democracy of the United States, and to make a good profit for the promoters.

The CMS and its allies in Britain pressed for annexation to forestall Wakefield's plans and the resulting harm they believed would come to Maori. The New Zealand Company rushed to establish a beachhead first. Its first shipload of settlers landed on the shores of Port Nicholson (Wellington Harbour) in January 1840, a fortnight before Lieutenant-Governor William Hobson, despatched from Britain to establish sovereignty over New Zealand and assisted by CMS missionaries, signed a treaty with local tribes at Waitangi in the Bay of Islands. Most historians consider that the treaty was regarded very differently by the chiefs who assented to it and the representatives of the Crown who drew it up. The latter considered that 'sovereignty' was being transferred, while the former had actually been asked in the Maori version to approve the establishment of a 'governorship'. There was general agreement, however, that the Crown recognised that 'the chiefs and tribes' of New Zealand had legal title to their lands.

The government of the colony moved shortly afterwards to Auckland. With very limited revenue and command over comparatively little armed force, it did not greatly impress either Maori or settler. Meanwhile Wakefield's project had continued apace, with thousands of additional colonists landing at Wellington, Nelson and New Plymouth (Taranaki). With few means of generating exports in the short term, these settlements tended to stagnate economically. However, the importation of flocks of sheep from Australia and the leasing from Maori of open grassland in the Wairarapa district, to the east of Wellington, pointed the way to development based on wool exports to Europe. A second wave of Wakefield settlements saw thousands more Europeans settle further south, in the Scottish Free Church settlement of Otago (1848) and the Anglican settlement of Canterbury (1850). Wool-growing proved the economic mainstay of those colonies as well.

In 1852 New Zealand was granted responsible government, with a legislature consisting of an elected House of Representatives and an upper Legislative Council appointed for life by the Governor. The country was divided into seven provinces (Auckland, Taranaki, Hawke's Bay, Wellington, Nelson, Canterbury and Otago), each with a Superintendent and an elected Provincial Council. Southland, Westland and Marlborough all later became provinces. Given the difficulties of communication between the main settlements, provincial interests and loyalties proved very strong in the House of Representatives. Each major province developed its own public works and immigration policy, and drew income from the sale of Crown land.

> It is a part of the aspirations of the Anglo-Saxon race to obtain land for themselves. It is that feeling which has brought us to the countries; it is that feeling that has made the British people successful in the work of colonisation; and that feeling should be fostered rather than discouraged.[1]
>
> WILLIAM MASSEY, 20 JULY 1894

The New Zealand wars

European settlement had a major impact on Maori society. On the one hand, it provided a market for agricultural produce, particularly in the Auckland region, and a conduit for trade to the booming goldfields of Australia. On the other hand, it brought pressure to sell communal land. This led to disputes over which Maori had the right to sell particular blocks of land, not just because of the money involved but also because the recognition of ownership conveyed *mana* to the sellers at the expense of other claimants. Resistance to this process in much of the North Island crystallised around the election of a Maori King, the leading Waikato chief Potatau. The existence of the Kingite movement, headquartered on the lower Waikato River, comparatively close to the developing Auckland settlement, was seen as a potential threat by some settlers, as a barrier to European purchase of much fertile land and as a challenge to the sovereignty of the Crown. In 1861 a dispute over whether a group of Maori in Taranaki had the right to sell a particular block of land near the main settlement of New Plymouth led to confrontation with the government and an outbreak of fighting. The involvement of Kingites from Waikato in the struggle presented the government with the opportunity to launch a military invasion of that area from Auckland. Several pitched battles ensued, generally centred on Maori *pa* (fortresses) equipped with entrenchments that protected the defenders from artillery fire and provided ample opportunities for ambushing attackers. In addition to the fighting in the Waikato district, there were major campaigns in the Bay of Plenty and Taranaki. The tenacity of Maori resistance and a number of incidents that were taken to reflect their adoption of Christian charity towards their enemies created a surprisingly positive attitude in the later European discussions of their opponents.

Defeat of the Kingites led to the withdrawal of the Maori King south into what became known as King Country, and confiscation by the government of extensive areas of Maori communal land in the Waikato district, Bay of Plenty and Taranaki. Partly as a result of the confiscations, a further wave of Maori unrest swept much of the North Island. This was often associated with a religious movement called *pai marire*, dubbed *hau hau* by the settler population. Some adherents of *pai marire* adopted older traditions, including cannibalism, and were regarded with horror by most Europeans. This was counterbalanced by the fact that on the government side much of the fighting was carried out by 'loyal' Maori, who objected to what they saw as challenges to their own tribal and personal *mana* by the followers of *pai marire*. The widespread perception of Maori amongst Europeans as inherently 'noble' was not therefore radically undermined, even when leaders of the 'loyal' tribes later objected to continued large-scale purchases of Maori communal land. However, most European New Zealanders, who lived in the main centres, had little contact with Maori, who lived mostly in rural areas of the North Island.

Economic development

Auckland initially gained from the wars of the 1860s, as the provisioning and accommodation of regular British regiments and local forces, many of them recruited from Australia, created a major market. There was also an assumption that the removal of Kingite control of the Waikato district would lead to rapid economic expansion. However, following the success of that campaign, the scale of operations was reduced, and fighting moved southwards to Taranaki and the North Island's east coast. In 1869 the last regiment of regular British troops was withdrawn despite continued Maori resistance, leading to some muttering in the colony about the possibility of breaking the imperial tie. While many soldiers in the New Zealand forces were provided with confiscated land, the hoped-for bonanza did not eventuate.

Furthermore, the real bonanza, the major discoveries of gold that boosted New Zealand's population enormously and drove much of its development in the 1860s and the decades thereafter, occurred in the South Island, principally in Otago and on the West Coast. Those areas were as likely to look to Australia as to Auckland for imports and services. Dunedin suddenly became the largest town in the country, and Otago its most populous province. A large proportion of the new-comers had been on the goldfields of Australia or even those of California earlier. They tended to bring with them a strong sense of democracy and, generally, a strong hostility towards Chinese immigrants, a few thousand of whom came to the New Zealand goldfields as they had gone to the other Pacific gold rushes. In 1865 New Zealand's capital was moved south to Wellington, partially reflecting the shift in the balance of the population, removing another source of economic activity from Auckland.

The South Island and the southern North Island were also to benefit disproportionately from the next great wave of development in New Zealand, the Vogel boom of the 1870s. In 1869 Julius Vogel, Colonial Treasurer, proposed that the New Zealand government should undertake large-scale borrowing in London to finance a major programme of immigration and public works. This would permit a rapid development of the country's resources that would supposedly more than cover the resulting burden of debt. Although there was a strategic element in the plan, looking to speed the movement of government forces to the site of any Maori unrest in the North Island, the greatest spending was in the South Island. That was where the bulk of the European population lived and where open plains provided the best opportunities for railway construction and agricultural development.

Thanks largely to the Vogel Scheme, the population of New Zealand doubled in a decade. Moreover, the predominance of young people amongst the immigrants led to something of a baby boom. While New Zealanders of Massey's age (he was born in 1856) tended to be born outside the country, a majority of adult New Zealanders were locally born before the end of the century.

This process was accentuated by the decrease in immigration during the 1880s and the first half of the 1890s as much of New Zealand suffered from the effects of the global 'long depression', which featured low prices for wool and restricted opportunities to borrow, particularly when the country was already heavily indebted. Evidence of net European emigration from the colony in some years proved particularly disturbing. However, the process of farm development continued, not least in rainforest areas of the Manawatu, Taranaki and Hawke's Bay, with settlers who possessed limited capital utilising their own labour and that of their families to clear the forest and establish pastures. Access to newly-built railways meant that more timber could be milled rather than simply burned. Following the first export of refrigerated produce to London in 1882 on the *Dunedin*,

The advent of refrigerated shipping transformed much of New Zealand's economy. In the 1870s the country's main exports consisted of wool and gold. Following news of successful shipments of frozen produce elsewhere, South Island business interests had the *Dunedin* fitted out to carry such produce, mostly sheepmeat, to Britain in 1882. After some initial difficulties, the trade in frozen meat, especially lamb, burgeoned. Many freezing works were established, particularly on railway lines close to the major port cities. The dairy industry grew more slowly, but cheese and butter had become major exports by 1900. Dairying and fat-lamb farming made smaller farms more economic, allowing individuals with less capital to get established. They were also particularly suited to wetter areas, especially the west and north of the North Island, reinforcing the 'drift' of population northwards.

a major new frozen meat industry developed quite rapidly, based principally on exports of lamb. The export of cheese and butter expanded more gradually. Although these industries were first established in the South Island, the higher rainfall, warmer winters and consequent greater pasture growth in most of the North Island meant that it was to gain disproportionately from them, and its population eventually overtook that of the South Island at the start of the new century.

'Recolonisation' and its limits

Most of the meat and dairy products exported went to the British market. Indeed these products, such as fatty lamb and cheddar cheese, were tailored to that market. This has led one prominent New Zealand historian, James Belich, to see refrigeration as a central element in what he terms the 'recolonisation' of the country, as its economy became increasingly focused on the British market. There were other features of New Zealand's settlement and situation that tended to reinforce the British link. Despite some significant Irish Catholic immigration during the New Zealand Wars, the gold rushes and the Vogel boom, the overwhelming majority of the European population was Protestant. Most of them were of English or Scottish origins, though a disproportionate and increasing minority came from the north of Ireland. Despite a continuing flow of arrivals from across the Tasman Sea, which became something of a flood during the gold rushes and wars of the 1860s, more immigrants tended to come directly from Britain on sailing ships, with no landfall, until the advent of more efficient long-distance steamship technology in the 1880s. There was also an uncomfortable perception that New Zealand, and indeed Australia, were relatively defenceless against attacks by other European powers (typically the Russians) or from Asia. The Royal Navy, the most powerful fleet in the world, was seen as the great guarantor of the colony's security.

Not that the New Zealand government considered itself subject to any decision the government in London might force upon it. In 1892 the Colonial Office ruled that the sovereign's representative in New Zealand, the Governor, must take the advice of his local ministers. This meant in effect that no military formations could be raised or financed in New Zealand without the concurrence of its government and ultimately its Parliament. It was not clear what the granting of the title 'Dominion' to New Zealand in 1907 meant constitutionally, but locally it was regarded as recognition that the country stood alongside Canada, Australia and South Africa on a very different plane from 'non-White' colonies.

One particular concern, particularly amongst working-class New Zealanders, was that an influx of 'non-White' immigrants might undermine their standards of living. Given that some thousands of Chinese had arrived in the gold rushes and that the vast population of China was perceived as dangerously close, it was Chinese immigration that was seen as particularly threatening. Hence Liberal Governments passed a raft of legislation aimed at deterring 'non-White' and especially Chinese immigrants. In addition to a dictation test in a European language, this included a progressively heavier charge on vessels carrying Chinese to New Zealand and the requirement that the arrivals should submit to thumb-printing to ensure that photo-identification was not undermined by the inability of European officials to distinguish between individual Chinese. While British governments were not necessarily unsympathetic, imperial interests in China and India meant that such actions by New Zealand

and the other 'White' Dominions caused some embarrass-
ment in London.

Conversely, the Anglo-Japanese alliance, concluded in
1902, occasioned some discomfort locally as tensions developed between Japan and the United States following the
former's victory in the Russo-Japanese War in 1905. The
growing European perception of a 'yellow peril' was strongly
felt in New Zealand, and the United States was viewed optimistically by many New Zealanders as a further bulwark
protecting them from Asian threats. That belief contributed
to an enthusiastic local welcome for the American President
Theodore Roosevelt's 'Great White Fleet' in 1908, when it
visited Auckland as part of its world tour. The following year
the New Zealand Prime Minister informed an Imperial Conference in London that if Britain went to war with the United
States in alliance with Japan, it might face 'a parting of the
ways' with New Zealand.

Political developments

Given the cost of emigrating as far as New Zealand, it is
perhaps unsurprising that the dominant ethos in its European society (and to a surprising degree amongst Maori) was
that of the individual or at least familial self-help that tended
to characterise the British 'middling sort'. The acquisition
of economic independence through land ownership, self-
employment and skill was highly valued, while a perceived
inclination to depend on official or private charity was dis-
paraged. It was widely held that the abundance of undevel-
oped resources and absence of aristocratic privilege in New
Zealand meant that all men should be able to make their own
way to independence. Certainly there should be no need for
poor laws that degraded individuals and burdened small as

well as large ratepayers in 'the Old Country'. On the other hand, there was a widespread sensitivity to the development of any barriers to advancement, such as the 'locking up' of land that would make it inaccessible to closer European settlement. There was a tendency to expect the government to remove such barriers and to assist development through the provision of infrastructure. As the leading New Zealand historian, Bill Oliver, remarked, this approach could be typified as favouring an 'enabling' rather than a 'welfare' state'.[2] It advocated intervention to assist men to achieve their independence through farming, trades and the purchase of property.

From at least the 1870s, there were political divisions between those who believed in greater or lesser state activity in promoting individual advancement. At one extreme it was argued that the market was operating efficiently in New Zealand, that the existence of large private landholdings reflected economic realities, and that state intervention and trade unionism represented threats to the country's development. At the other extreme, some politicians, most notably John Ballance, believed that land nationalisation would ultimately be necessary to prevent an all-powerful landlord class from emerging and blocking access to the settlement of ordinary New Zealanders on farms. Another set of ideas that gained some currency were those of the writer Henry George. He maintained that landowners gained an 'unearned increment' when the values of their holdings went up due to government spending on infrastructure. A 'single tax' to capture that increase in value could replace all other taxes, which inhibited enterprise, and provide the basis for further state investment in infrastructure. Those who favoured greater state intervention somewhat paradoxically adopted the title

'Liberal' for their movement, though their opponents continued to argue that they themselves were 'the true Liberals'.

The Liberal government

Led by John Ballance, the Liberals came to power in 1891, following what turned out to be a narrow victory in the general election at the end of the previous year. The most prominent issue in that election appears to have been their promise to replace the existing property tax with a graduated land tax that many believed would serve to 'burst up the great estates' that were seen as standing in the way of closer settlement. Compulsory purchase of some of those estates for subdivision was also foreshadowed, together with a move towards more leasing rather than selling of Crown land. While the land tax was not in practice set at levels likely to force large landowners to sell their estates, the government did purchase and subdivide Cheviot, a big holding in northern Canterbury. This and the prospect of further such actions appear to have underwritten a great Liberal victory, particularly in rural areas, at the end of 1893.

Meanwhile, a basis for trade union activity had grown with the development of large workplaces such as ports, coal mines, railway workshops, meat-processing works and factories producing consumer goods for an increasingly integrated New Zealand market. There were surges in labour organising in the 1870s and again in the late 1880s, most strongly centred on the waterfront, shipping and coal-mining. In 1890 their umbrella organisation, the Maritime Council, was defeated in a dispute with ship owners. However, five 'Labour' representatives gained seats in the subsequent general election and many of the victorious Liberals had pledged support for trade unionism. Measures promoted by the new government included the introduction of compulsory arbitration between trade unions and groups of employers. A Department of Labour was created partly to police legislation designed to improve working conditions.

The Liberals were led to victory in 1893 by Richard Seddon, following Ballance's death earlier in the year. Seddon enjoyed great popular support, but was regarded by his opponents as common and corrupt. He proceeded with the implementation of compulsory arbitration, which was to have the effect of promoting the rapid growth of a myriad of predominantly small trade unions able to advance the pay and conditions of their members through the Arbitration Court rather than industrial action. However, Seddon's awareness of the discontent of many Liberal-voting farmers and business-people with increasing regulations contributed to his decision to call a virtual halt to 'experimental labour legislation'.

The purchase and subdivision of large estates continued and was more than matched by the buying of Maori communal land, particularly in the North Island; borrowing in London was resumed, initially to finance 'Advances to Settlers', loans at comparatively low rates of interest to enable farmers to get established on new holdings that initially provided little income. Substantial borrowing for public works and strong growth in the global economy from the mid-1890s also helped Seddon to pile up large majorities in successive general elections. Nor did the Liberals neglect their working-class constituency, establishing technical colleges to provide young workers with the skills to gain their independence and Advances to Workers to assist them to establish themselves in their own homes. Miles Fairburn argues that the latter move in particular permitted a reconciliation between the dominant rural myth on the one hand, which held that working a family farm was the personal and social ideal, and the reality, on the other hand, that employment was increasingly urban. He maintains that it did so by placing workers on little suburban farms, where they could raise their own vegetables and fowls, while commuting to work.

At the beginning of the 20th century New Zealand had an international reputation as a 'social laboratory' for experiments in state intervention, thanks largely to the Liberals' legislation. In 1893 the House of Representatives had voted overwhelmingly to make New Zealand the first country to extend the franchise to women. It was also comparatively wealthy and technologically advanced, with its first cinema opening less than two years after that of the Lumière brothers in Paris, and a local pioneer of powered aviation succeeding in getting airborne, albeit not in a particularly controlled manner, before the Wright brothers. Real wages tended to be higher than in Europe, particularly for skilled workers in the towns. The local councils of the main cities, and quite a number of smaller towns, tended to take much the same pride in municipal buildings and services as their counterparts in British cities. There was a widespread belief in the value and inevitability of technological and material progress, and various 'advanced' ideas, including socialism and experiments in

Richard John Seddon ('King Dick') was born in Lancashire in 1845. Having served an apprenticeship as a mechanical engineer, he emigrated to Australia, where he worked in railway workshops and did some gold mining. In 1866 he moved to the diggings on the west coast of the South Island, becoming established as a miner, publican, miners' legal agent and local politician. In 1879 he became an MP and in 1891 a minister in the Liberal Government. Responsibility for public works enabled him to develop a political following throughout the country and in 1893 he outmanoeuvred his opponents to become Premier. A mighty orator with 'the common touch', he dominated New Zealand's politics until his death in 1906.

communitarianism, were discussed, even if only a small minority embraced them.

Prohibition was an issue that brought together many religious conservatives, most of them Protestant, particularly from non-conformist denominations, and a substantial number of progressives. From 1893 it was possible for 60 per cent of voters in a constituency to force the elimination of licensed premises in their area, so long as at least half the registered electors voted. A significant number of areas subsequently became 'dry'. At the 1902, 1905, 1908 and 1911 elections there was a majority nationally for prohibition, but the 60 per cent requirement prevented its introduction. Popular radical politicians like Tommy Taylor in Christchurch were strong prohibitionists.

The rise of the Reform Party
Seddon's death in 1906 brought Sir Joseph Ward to power. Ward was never as popular as Seddon and was somewhat vulnerable because his business investments had helped provoke a banking crisis and his own bankruptcy in the mid-1890s. He was also a Catholic at a time when sectarian issues were on the rise, and his acceptance of a baronetcy exposed him to some derision. Above all, however, he faced some new challenges. One of these was the rise of syndicalism – the belief amongst many union activists that direct action was the means by which workers' interests were best advanced and a general strike the way in which capitalism could be overthrown. At the same time the view that no further Crown land should be sold and even that land should be nationalised was expressed by some, mainly urban, Liberals.

Such ideas, and the return of strikes, were anathema to many New Zealanders, particularly in rural areas. In response to the Liberals' constituency amongst Maori and to the perception that many Maori might become pauperised if too much of their land was sold, the Liberal Government had favoured the long-term leasing rather than outright purchase of such land. This offended many would-be settlers and townspeople, particularly in the northern North Island, who believed they would benefit from closer European settlement. On top of this, New Zealand was affected by a world recession from 1909. While working-class voters, particularly in urban areas, remained relatively loyal to the Liberals, there was a considerable splintering of their rural support, which eventually led to their defeat by Massey's Reform Party in the House of Representatives in 1912.

However, Ward and the Liberals did suffer some loss of working-class support to independent labour groups, which won four seats at the 1911 election. One policy that contributed to this development was the decision to introduce compulsory military training for young men in their teens and early twenties under the 1909 Defence Act. That move, together with the financing of the building of a dreadnought for the Royal Navy, was part of the Government's response to calls for the Empire to provide more assistance to the United Kingdom

Joseph George Ward was born in Melbourne in 1856, coming to New Zealand in 1863 with his widowed mother, an astute businesswoman. He became a produce merchant, shipping agent and seller of farm supplies. After holding local body offices, he became MP for Awarua in 1887, Postmaster-General in the Liberal Government in 1891 and Colonial Treasurer in 1893. He gained enormous kudos in 1895 for borrowing £1.5 million in London at low interest to finance Advances to Settlers. Ward overcame personal bankruptcy in 1897, returned rapidly to politics, was knighted in 1901 and became Prime Minister in 1906. He was made a Baronet in 1911. After resigning in 1912, he was again leading the Opposition in 1913, but lost his seat in 1919. Back in Parliament in 1925, he led a minority government from 1928 to just before his death in 1930.

in carrying the burden of imperial defence at a time when German naval construction was seen as posing a serious challenge. Even during the patriotic fervour that accompanied New Zealand's participation in the Boer War, some voices had been raised against it. Now the use of compulsion to force young New Zealanders into military camps and potentially overseas to fight came up against strong opposition, not least in Christchurch. Over a hundred defaulters were convicted and served sentences in ordinary prisons, despite being generally from very respectable, typically church-going families. The change of government in 1912 saw a hardening of attitudes on either side. Reform was more diligent in pursuing defaulters and deducted fines from their wages. Replacement of prison sentences with military detention did little to calm opponents, and five young Christchurch men imprisoned at the military base on Ripa Island were widely acclaimed as heroes after enduring a regime of sub-standard food and indecent language.

The country of which Massey was now to be Prime Minister and which he was to lead into the First World War identified strongly with its British heritage while seeing itself as more healthy, egalitarian and progressive than 'the Old Country' – a 'better Britain', as historian James Belich has characterised its self-perception. While most economic activity was directed at an internal market, exports, particularly of wool, meat and dairy products, were disproportionately important. Most of those exports went to Britain, and a rather smaller proportion of imports came from there. Both overseas borrowing and direct investment was from Britain. Despite the existence of a significant Maori minority, much of it disaffected in the process of colonisation, the overwhelming majority of the population saw the Dominion as very much a 'white' country, permanently separated from Asia, if uncomfortably close to it. It was far from being an entirely united society; a largely urban minority rejected the dominant capitalist system and looked to the establishment of socialism. Some of that minority drew much of their inspiration from North America and the radical Industrial Workers of the World (IWW) that flourished there, but the strongest element looked to British and European socialism. In turn, devotion to socialism not infrequently overlapped with the discontents of the minority of the population of Irish Catholic origin.

2

Massey's Life to 1914

William (Bill) Ferguson Massey was born in the small town of Limavady in County Londonderry in the Irish province of Ulster on 26 March 1856. His family could accurately be described as Ulster Scots, with his father from a long-established local Presbyterian family and his mother born in Scotland itself. John and Mary Anne Massey were of modest means, with a smallholding of around ten acres and a small area of leased land. In 1862 they chose to follow the example of generations of Irish Protestants before them and emigrate. However, rather than set out for the most common, and the cheapest, destination of North America, they embarked for the 'farthest promised land' of New Zealand.[1] The sale of their freehold and tenancy presumably paid for their fares and those of their two younger children. One attraction in emigrating to New Zealand was the Auckland Provincial Government's offer of 40 acres freehold to adult immigrants who paid their own passage, with an additional 20 acres for each child. Bill was left behind with his grandparents and other relatives to complete his primary education at the Limavady National School and to obtain some secondary education privately.

Early influences

Less than a year before his death, Bill Massey was to recall how reading the Bible had featured in his education in Limavady, laying the foundation for the numerous references that were to sprinkle his speeches:

> *When I was a boy I had the opportunity of learning as much about the Bible as most people. I attended a school at which the Bible was read in the morning, and where if any of the pupils chose to come together for an hour on Saturday mornings to receive religious teaching they had the opportunity of doing so ... Later on, when I went to a secondary school connected with the same organisation, the proceedings were slightly different. After the school opened in the morning the boys of the senior class read from the French Testament verse by verse and translated. ... We had amongst us boys from Church of England, Presbyterian, Roman Catholic, Wesleyan, and other denominations – the children of the people of the district. We were practically all of the same way of thinking. Those who chose to have Bible-reading attended the class; those who did not stayed away.*[2]

Another text that Massey read at school was published by the Chambers Educational Series shortly after 1848 and dealt with political economy. His first biographer considered that few of the Prime Minister's opinions had been influenced by the constitutionally conservative and economically free-trade ideas embodied in the schoolbook. However, the emphases on individual duty, economic independence and the folly of government interference in the marketplace were all to find an echo in Massey's later political rhetoric.[3] During one of his two visits back to Limavady in his adult life, a former schoolmate remembered Massey as exceptionally good at sums and eager to demonstrate it by solving those set for other children.

'Farmer Bill'

The Masseys' section of New Zealand was at Puhoi, then a comparatively isolated bush settlement near the river of that name on the east coast north of Auckland town. Isolation and rather unpromising soil combined to make it generally unattractive for profitable farming. Indeed a corruption of the word Puhoi became a by-word in the Auckland region for a predicament or unpleasant situation, rendered as 'up the Boo-ai'. Certainly the Masseys were greatly disappointed with their section, soon moving to leased land at West Tamaki, closer to the town of Auckland.

It was there that Bill, then fourteen, joined them in December 1870, travelling with a neighbour of the Masseys' who had returned to Scotland to visit relatives. For the next three years Bill worked with his father on the farm at West Tamaki, although the property was not particularly productive. Between 1873 and 1876 he gained some experience of the rapid agricultural development that was occurring in the South Island when he worked on the estate of John Grigg at Longbeach, near Ashburton in Canterbury. Grigg had been a neighbour of the Masseys before moving south. He was known as a particularly progressive landowner and invested heavily in drainage work to develop his estate. Horse-drawn and increasingly steam-powered machinery was used on such large farms, particularly in grain-growing. According to a story Massey later told, he once instructed the driver of a traction engine he was on to break the law by driving the machine on the railway bridge across the Ashburton River rather than over the flooded riverbed. Subsequently he took responsibility for the transgression, pleaded guilty and paid the fine of one pound, then a not inconsiderable sum. The incident suggests that despite his young age Massey was issuing orders and expecting them to be obeyed, but that he was also prepared to take the consequences.

Massey was to refer to his comparatively impecunious early life frequently during his later political career. Indeed he mouthed references to an absence of an inherited 'silver spoon' all too often. Yet he appears to have been genuine in believing that this gave him a special sympathy for those facing poverty, as during the depression of 1921–2: *I was not born with a silver spoon in my mouth. I have been through the mill, and I know where my sympathies are … My sympathies are with the under dog; and there are plenty of people who require assistance at the present time, and we are going to help them as I suggested.*[4] Likewise, when in power he followed Seddon, but not Ward, in declining a knighthood or title. Challenged two years before his death as to whether a 'Lord Massey' was possible, he declared *I have resisted temptation up to the present, and I hope that I shall be able to resist it to the end.*[5]

There were repeated suggestions that he had joined the radical Knights of Labor during his youth. He denied it towards the end of his life, claiming that he had merely accepted the support of its local members in his early move into politics. He had said the same thing in a speech at Gisborne in 1908, citing it as evidence that he had the support of working men.[6] However, the Knights of Labor were democratic but not socialist in their doctrines, and the organisation had many of the trappings of a Masonic lodge about it.

Like many Protestants of his generation, Massey was quite an enthusiast for such lodges.

After rejoining his parents, who were now farming at Mangere, a district south of the town of Auckland, Bill leased 100 acres in the same area. Despite its relatively high rainfall, significant quantities of grain were grown in Auckland Province at the time, and he purchased a steam-driven machine to thresh crops on contract. In 1882, at the age of 26, he was sufficiently well established to marry Christina Allan Paul, the daughter of a neighbouring farming family originally from Scotland. Massey later claimed to have been *somewhat of an athlete myself up to twenty-five years of age*, suggesting that he gave up participation in sports around the time he assumed family responsibilities.[7] Four sons and three daughters were born in the next ten years.

By the end of the 1880s he was farming a very respectable 300 acres in Mangere. He had also become a pillar of the local community, chairing its school committee and serving on the Mangere Road Board. Massey was the first Chairman of the Mangere Farmers' Club and became President of the Auckland Agricultural and Pastoral Association. He was a member of the Orange Institution and briefly became its

Married at nineteen, Christina Allan Massey maintained the family household in Mangere, bringing up five children while being active in local associations. A further two children died in infancy. She moved to Wellington when her husband became Prime Minister in 1912. As well as being the hostess at gatherings in the official residence, she took leadership roles in several national organisations, most notably as President of the Plunket Society, which aimed to improve the care of mothers and babies. She accompanied Bill on his visits to Europe to attend the 1917 and 1921 Imperial Conferences and the Paris Peace Conference. After contracting influenza during the 1918 epidemic, she suffered ill-health for the rest of her life. She was made a Dame of the Grand Cross of the British Empire in 1926 and died in 1932.

Grand Master for the North Island in 1892.[8] However, his membership of the Masonic Order itself was more enduring and he was to be the Grand Master for New Zealand at the time he died. He was also a member of the Oddfellows.

The move into politics

As a prominent, relatively youthful farmer living in a rapidly developing area not far from Auckland city, Bill Massey was invited in September 1891 to participate in the formation of a 'National Association' to oppose the recently elected Liberal Government. The leadership of the Association, which failed to become established outside Auckland, was dominated by city businessmen, but Massey was elected its vice-president. He stood unsuccessfully for the opposition in his local electorate of Franklin (then often spelt 'Franklyn') at the 1893 general election, despite a newspaper that supported his opponent describing him as 'a popular and esteemed man'.[9]

However, the following year he was successful in a by-election for neighbouring Waitemata, when the opposition member there was disqualified after a court ruled that his supporters had 'treated' voters during the general election. The way Massey received the invitation from opposition supporters to stand for the seat has become an indelible part of his image as 'Farmer Bill'. He was apparently on top of a stack and it was handed up to him on the end of a pitchfork. In 1896 he stood again in Franklin and defeated the Liberal MP there. In his two years as MP for Waitemata, Massey had won over even a Liberal-supporting newspaper: 'Mr Massey … has been a live [sic] Member, full of energy and life, and fully alive to the interests of this part of the Colony and untiring in his efforts to promote them. He has, in a word, been one of our best Members. We would have liked him better if he had been on the Government side of the House, but no matter which side he is on, Mr Massey is a rattling good fellow, Liberal in his political convictions, and worthy of a seat in Parliament for any country constituency' [10]

As W J Gardner later pointed out, Massey's popularity was built in large part on his success as an advocate for local interests, not least in securing funds for public works. Thus he ended his short term as MP for Waitemata by declaring proudly that *Though he was not a follower of the present Government, he was enabled to get £4,800 for roads and bridges, and £8,000 for railways in the Waitemata electorate.* [11] In the subsequent contest at Franklin 'the subject of liveliest debate in the campaign was the question whether his opponent or himself should get the credit for two local grants of £250 and £200. Deference to localism could hardly go further.' [12] Massey was to hold the Franklin seat for the rest of his life, enjoying large majorities. This reflected both the increasingly prosperous and settled nature of the electorate and his continued diligence as a local member. In 1905 Seddon paid him the dubious compliment of holding five meetings in Franklin while Massey campaigned elsewhere.

Seddon's capacity to relate warmly to individuals and to remember their names and concerns was undoubtedly a significant part of his popular appeal, especially in rural and small-town New Zealand. Massey certainly had that capacity as well. Like 'King Dick' he was always quick to remark how well the crops and livestock were looking in the localities he visited, though Massey in Opposition was inclined to imply that this was particularly praiseworthy in light of the Government's neglect of the district's interests. It is possible that such compliments carried a little more weight coming from a farmer rather than a publican.

Massey entered Parliament with a strong belief in the values of manly independence that were so widespread in New Zealand society. He saw his own relative success as exemplifying the worth of such values:

> *I have invariably found that the man who comes out best in the long-run is the self-reliant man. I mean, the man who ceases, when the opportunity offers, to be a worker in the ordinary acceptation of the term; and I know as much about the difficulties of the worker as most people. Speaking personally, all that I started with was this: I inherited a good constitution, and I still possess it. My parents were not possessed of much of this world's goods. All they were able to give me was a sound education, and at twenty-one I was in business for myself. I am convinced that any one can do that; it is within the reach of all. If the workers would endeavour to improve their position, and endeavour, above all things, to provide homes for themselves, they would become independent.*[13]

The issues stressed in Massey's earliest electoral contests were to be those he emphasised in Parliament and on the hustings throughout most of his time in opposition. He condemned the Liberal emphasis on providing leasehold rather than freehold farms to settlers as creating a 'State landlordism' at least as bad as the aristocratic landlordism of the Old World. Likewise he never accepted the arguments of John Stuart Mill or Henry George that increased land values were the product of investment by the community: *Any one who talks about community-created values forgets the women and children who are working hard in our out-districts improving the land on which they live … It is not community-created value, but it is industry-created value, and the industry is the industry of the settlers.*[14]

For much of his political career Massey reflected the discontent of many people in the former Auckland Province, especially but certainly not exclusively in rural areas, who assumed the Liberal Government favoured the South Island.

[I]t is a question of serfs of the Crown or every man his own landlord.[15]

WILLIAM MASSEY, 4 SEPTEMBER 1906

Aucklanders generally agreed with his charges that too much money was being spent on purchasing land from European owners in the South Island and on developing infrastructure there, to the detriment of further purchases of Maori communal land and progress in road-building in the north of the North Island.

Massey was relentless in opposition, bringing a single-minded dedication to the task of criticising and embarrassing the Government. Although Parliament generally sat in winter, when agricultural activity tended to be at its lowest ebb, the session continued into spring and early summer, and the new MP was to find that juggling his responsibilities as a farmer and rural businessmen with those of a politician posed great difficulties. As he admitted late in life: *My own experience, although I am out of business as an agriculturalist at the present time, is that unless the settler himself is at the head of affairs in agricultural and pastoral operations they are not carried on as well as otherwise would be the case. They used to tell me – and I found it out in my personal experience – that farming and politics do not go together.*[16]

The need to travel to Wellington when Parliament was sitting made the supervision of his farming and contracting interests difficult, and brought separation from his young family. It is clear that he decided that if he were to make the sacrifices necessary for a man of his limited means to pursue a career in politics, there would be no half-measures. Seddon drove Parliament hard, as Massey was to recall later: *on one occasion I was on a Committee, the House used to sit until seven o'clock in the morning towards the end of the session, and we would be back at half past ten in our places in the House.*[17]

Massey became Opposition Whip in 1896 and repeatedly disputed the Government's management of the House. He later admitted that his side of the House had indulged in *stonewalling and abuse* under his direction.[18] Speaking numerous times each session, he stood out in an Opposition whose members were often from much wealthier, indeed leisured, backgrounds. Certainly by the time of the 1899 general election the main newspaper supporting the Opposition in Auckland was claiming that Massey was the MP Seddon would most like to see unseated.

Leader of the opposition

In 1901 Sir William Russell, the large Hawke's Bay landowner who had led the Opposition since 1899, decided to step down from the leadership. He was not replaced for over two years, despite the Opposition having to fight an election in 1902. To a large extent Massey came to play the role of leader through management of his side of the House. This, together with the support of some new members more determined to try to overthrow the Liberal Government, saw him elected unopposed as Leader of the Opposition in September 1903.

Massey brought his usual energy and determination to his new task. Before the 1905 general election he ventured on a speaking tour of the South Island, seeking to broaden the Opposition's geographical base. He pitted himself deliberately against Seddon himself, following the Premier as the latter pursued his usual punishing schedule of speeches throughout the country. The result gave relatively little comfort to the Opposition, but it certainly cemented Massey's status as its unquestioned leader.

The death of Seddon in early 1906 and his replacement with Sir Joseph Ward presented Massey with a much more promising target. He was in campaign mode more than a year before the next election. Entertained by supporters at Hawera in southern Taranaki:

> *He wanted to say that it was not the slightest use the Chairman paying him compliments and the other gentlemen attending his banquet unless these meetings were followed by practical results … Speaking from a party point of view, it was the duty of the Opposition to criticise the proposals of the Government. This was considered to be the function of the Opposition at Home, but the present New Zealand Opposition party had gone much further … He then referred to various measures that the Opposition had brought forward … and the Government had taken credit for. This should be a complete answer to those who said the Opposition was the remnant of the old Tory party and were Conservatives … The Opposition wanted to see more done for the pioneer settler, to have the Civil Service put on a proper footing, and to see an elective Legislative Council.[19]*

Massey played a major role in making the Opposition

more electable. He tightened up its discipline and obliged his fellow leaders, most of them of much higher social status than himself, to campaign throughout the country as he did. In 1909 he had what was already in effect a party adopt the more positive title of Reform, in recognition of the success of some Opposition supporters in forming Political Reform Leagues in various parts of the country. The name resonated with perceptions that government had become corrupt under the Liberals, perceptions that were not limited to the Opposition's supporters. The Christchurch radical MP and Mayor, Tommy Taylor, had devoted much of his parliamentary career to denouncing what he called

> **Those who were alarmed at the spread of Socialism should assist the party that had stood up, with a certain amount of success, against Socialistic proposals in Parliament.**[20]
> **WILLIAM MASSEY, 30 APRIL 1908**

'Tammanyism' in New Zealand politics. A promise to make the Legislative Council, New Zealand's upper house, elected rather than appointed appealed to those who perceived the Council as a retirement home for loyal, if frequently undistinguished, supporters of whatever Government was in power.

These attacks on 'corruption' by the Liberal Government to some extent dovetailed with a surge of sectarian feeling in New Zealand. Government employment was widely sought after as a means of gaining a steady and safe remuneration in an economy where seasonal fluctuations could bring periods of unemployment or underemployment. Universal education since the 1870s meant there were many young people with sufficient literacy and numeracy to seek white-collar jobs, while the Liberals had expanded the scope of government by establishing several new ministries. The fact that Joseph Ward, a devout Catholic, was Postmaster-General at a time when postal services were expanding rapidly made for accusations that he was favouring his co-religionists. Indeed it was to become a truism in very many Protestant households throughout the 20th century that Catholics were disproportionately represented in the public service as a whole and that Catholic managers ensured that this remained the case. The growth in accusations that Ward had 'stacked' the public service with Catholics coincided with the establishment of the Catholic Federation, which pressed for more state assistance to denominational schools. Most provoking for many Protestants was the promulgation of the Papal decree *Ne Temere* in 1908. It ruled that marriages between Catholics and non-Catholics were not valid unless a priest officiated at the wedding. This was widely taken by Protestants to imply that mixed marriages not celebrated in this way were not true marriages, and any children of the union were illegitimate. The concomitant pressure to ensure that children of a mixed marriage contracted in a Catholic church should be raised in the faith was seen by many Protestants as a means to weaken Protestantism by taking over children who might otherwise continue in the religious identity of their non-Catholic parent and grandparents.

The MPs of the Reform Party were almost exclusively Protestant, and some were certainly members of the Orange Order. With his background in that Order, few Protestants had any doubt that Massey would oppose undue Catholic encroachment on government if he gained power. However, it is not evident that he sought to play on Protestant fears except insomuch as his criticisms of corruption in administration could be seen, as indeed many on both sides did see them, as coded references to sectarian favouritism. He certainly avoided raising such issues openly. Indeed, there is some evidence he believed that to do so would needlessly alienate Catholic voters. While the latter were very much a minority, Reform could not afford to write off 14 per cent of the electorate, many of them small farmers who might otherwise be attracted by its policies. Even in his own constituency, Massey was anxious that Catholics should not be driven away. His reference to his *Catholic friends* in a letter written to his political colleague Francis Fisher in 1910, suggests that he had good personal relationships with them. [21]

In seeking to attract potential voters away from the Liberal Party, Massey above all made it very clear that Reform was not going to dismantle the 'enabling state' built up by the Liberals, but was going to run it more honestly and efficiently. In 1908 he declared that he *favoured State assistance to industries but not State enterprise in place of private enterprise.*[22] By the time of the 1911 general election he was even proposing extensions in state intervention, including reducing the age of eligibility for the Old Age Pension for women from 65 to 60, and introducing compulsory sickness and unemployment insurance.

Before the 1905 election, a Christchurch newspaper that supported the Opposition had effectively resigned itself to defeat: 'The fact is the stars in their courses have fought for Seddon. He has had wondrous luck all along, and the present prosperous times are in his favour. When times are bad changes of Government are frequent. While things are good the people will not ask for Massey. They may want to change the family doctor when they feel ill. At present they don't feel a bit that way.' [23]

By the 1911 election, the stars had realigned themselves much more to Massey's advantage. In 1909 there was a severe downturn in world prices for the commodities New Zealand exported and a consequent contraction in the local economy. Government revenues fell, obliging it to curtail its spending and to lay off many public servants. Unemployment rose to levels not seen since the early 1900s. Here was an ideal opportunity for Massey to present himself as the country's GP, ready and able to treat its ailments. Moreover, while he was certainly not proposing the sort of largesse the *Spectator* had sarcastically recommended as the means to court electoral success, he was not advocating a return to a thin pre-Liberal diet. Indeed the patient was being encouraged to eat more heartily and was provided with a broad spread of policies, not just 'scraps'.

As another part of his single-minded drive to defeat Ward in 1911, Massey was prepared to make arrangements with candidates not pledged to Reform, generally from various Labour groupings that were disillusioned with the Liberal Government. The Second Ballot increased the opportunity to make such arrangements, typically through Reform candidates unsuccessful in the first round of voting agreeing to urge their supporters to vote for the anti-government candidate in the second round. In four cases the latter were elected, depriving Ward of his majority. When three of them effectively reneged on their agreement and did not vote for his no-confidence motion, Massey lost his temper and made unsubstantiated accusations against one of them that he had been bought off by the Liberals, accusations he was obliged to withdraw.

Nevertheless, the need for the Liberal Government, now led by the conservative erstwhile supporter of the Opposition Thomas Mackenzie, to keep its radical wing and the Labour members content proved to be its downfall. The latter groups were never going to approve easier extension of the freehold to state leaseholders and sufficient Liberal supporters of the freehold were eventually prepared to cross the floor to bring the Government down on 5 July 1912. Reform MPs cheered, but when Massey raised his hand they fell silent. Despite his relative lack of education and modest income, he was clearly the master of the party that included some of the best educated and wealthiest people in New Zealand.

Prime Minister

In government Massey moved to implement the promises Reform had made. There was no wholesale selling off of Crown land at giveaway prices, as the Liberals had alleged would happen, but freeholding by existing tenants was made easier. A Public Service Commission was established to put the appointment of public servants beyond the immediate reach of politicians. The House of Representatives agreed that the Legislative Council would be made elective under a system of Single Transferable Vote, with the country divided into two giant multi-member electorates. It was arguably only the advent of the First World War that prevented this innovation from coming into operation.

However, the first Reform Government is most widely associated in the New Zealand popular memory for the manner in which it carried out its promise to take a strong line against industrial unrest, which certainly did not abate with the coming to power of a party associated in the minds of most militants with the interests of the employers. It inherited a major dispute at the Waihi gold-mine, where the 'Red Fed' union was striking until their employers dismissed members of a newly formed engine-drivers union that was prepared to accept the arbitration system. The company involved may have welcomed the opportunity to break the militant union at a time when profitability of the mine was declining. It certainly moved to recruit strikebreakers, who were protected by the police. The strikebreakers responded increasingly violently to the active hostility of the strikers and eventually drove them from the town with the acquiescence of the police.

Massey faced a much greater threat in 1913 when disputes on the Wellington waterfront and at a coal mine in the Waikato escalated into a general strike. As during the 1890 Maritime Strike, the shipowners employed strikebreakers to operate the wharves. This time, however, it was clear that the 'Red Feds' were not going to limit themselves to peaceful picketing and demonstration marches. The government therefore mobilised large numbers of special constables to protect the strikebreakers and keep the wharves open. Both foot and mounted constables were deployed, but it was the latter that earned a place in New Zealand folklore. Generally recruited from rural areas, often through the newly organised network of territorial military units, they entered the main port cities in columns and established camps. In a number of cases, most notably in Lambton Quay in the heart of Wellington, they charged crowds taunting them. For many New Zealanders the memory of 'Massey's Cossacks', named by their opponents after the cavalry of the Russian autocracy, is one of the few things they associate with Bill Massey's rule.

While Massey was vilified by those sympathetic to the militants, there was a wider constituency formerly wary of a return to power of anti-Liberal forces that was pleasantly surprised at the way the Reform Government had largely adopted Liberal policies. When Massey made his first visit to Greymouth almost two years after taking office (the lengthy delay itself possibly indicative of the area's staunch Liberal and Labour identity), the Mayor welcomed him by remarking that 'They were not a conservative government (applause), and he was convinced that Mr. Massey was not of a conservative character.' [24]

Despite his long apprenticeship in opposition, Massey was very much a newly minted Prime Minister in August 1914. Although having previously shown little interest in foreign affairs and never having been out of New Zealand in his adult life, Massey was now to find himself the leader of a country at war and obliged to represent its interests in international forums.

3

New Zealand's Great War

The First World War had a profound impact on New Zealand and dominated the rest of Massey's time as Prime Minister – in effect, the rest of his life. Although the rate of deaths among New Zealander men of military age was far lower than in Britain, it was higher than in the other Dominions. This partly reflected the fact that, alone amongst them, New Zealand followed Britain in introducing conscription on a large scale. However, it mainly arose from the high level of volunteering locally. A large majority of New Zealanders who served in the war were volunteers, and many felt that some stigma was attached to waiting to be conscripted.

The toll

While a surprising number of mothers, wives and sisters of New Zealanders serving were able to afford to go to Britain, often performing war work there, for most relatives and friends left at home an extra layer of anxiety and loss was added by the fact that wounded or ill New Zealanders could not generally be visited while in hospital. Furthermore, a return home on leave was virtually impossible, and death invariably meant that there was no body to mourn over. For the families of those serving distance lent little enchantment.

Several MPs lost sons, including the Minister of Defence, James Allen. The following year Allen wrote to Major General Alexander John Godley, who commanded the New Zealand Expeditionary Force, 'Of course we grieve over our losses and simply have to bottle up our grief.'[1] W H D Bell MP, the son of Sir Francis Dillon Bell, who led the Reform Party in the Legislative Council, was killed in July 1917. Like many other New Zealanders, he was serving in a British regiment.

The youngest of Massey's three sons, George, volunteered in April 1915, serving initially as a private before being commissioned in October. He became Adjutant of the Second Battalion of the New Zealand Rifle Brigade and in 1917 was attached to an Ulster battalion of the Royal Irish Regiment, as part of a scheme to give New Zealand officers experience in staff work by serving temporarily with British brigades, gaining a Military Cross serving with the regiment at Messines. According to Sir James Allen, George's superiors did not know that he was the son of the Prime Minister until the New Zealand authorities told them. While serving as a major in

James Allen was born in Australia in 1855 and educated in Britain. At 22 he settled in Dunedin, where his father had accumulated considerable property. Allen served as a conservative MP from 1887 to 1890 and from 1892 to 1920. Valued for his reliability and practicality rather than dynamism or warmth, he was never likely to beat Massey to the leadership of the Opposition. In 1912 Allen took the Defence portfolio in addition to Finance and Education. He was instrumental in preparing the New Zealand Expeditionary Force, organising its reinforcement, implementing conscription and dealing with wartime discontent while Massey was overseas. In 1920 he became New Zealand High Commissioner in London and representative at the League of Nations. Knighted in 1917, he died in 1942 after serving in the Legislative Council from 1927 to 1941.

the Lancashire Fusiliers in March 1918, George was wounded in the fierce fighting occasioned by the German offensive.[2] Initially declared a hopeless case, a surgeon removed the bullet that had passed through both his lungs, which had apparently been sufficiently deflected by a buckle on his braces to miss his heart.[3]

At the same time as he endured the daily anxiety of what might happen to his son, the Prime Minister was faced with intractable economic and political problems within New Zealand itself and internationally. Speaking to Parliament in 1917 he maintained that *since the war broke out the business of Cabinet, especially with respect to industrial and commercial matters, has been multiplied by six. On one Sunday in particular I had thirty-one cables from London to deal with. I am bound to say that was a record day, but never a day passes without over twenty requiring attention.*[4]

Massey found himself having to consider decisions with profound implications for the lives of New Zealanders and the future of the Dominion. While he generally believed that the interests of Britain and New Zealand were identical, there were repeated instances when Massey considered those of the latter were being unduly sacrificed. At those times, he weighed in on the side of New Zealand.

Early months of war
Britain declared war on Germany on behalf of the British Empire on 4 August 1914. The New Zealand Government accepted without question that this meant it was now at war and the telegram from London advising of the declaration was read by the Governor, Lord Liverpool, on the steps of Parliament. A crowd estimated at 15,000, equivalent to about a fifth of the population of Wellington, heard Massey and

Ward pledge their parties to support the struggle and there was a massed singing of the National Anthem ('God Save the King'). Some scenes of patriotic enthusiasm ensued in centres throughout New Zealand and 14,000 men volunteered in the subsequent week. However, there was also widespread trepidation at what war might bring. On 3 August one provincial newspaper used giant headlines to ask 'Is It Armageddon?'[5]

The first action undertaken by New Zealand forces was launched less than a fortnight after the declaration of war. It came in response to a cable from the British Secretary of State for War intimating that 'If your Ministers desire and feel themselves

> **All we are and all we have are at the disposal of the Imperial Government for the purposes of carrying on the war to a successful issue.**[6]
>
> **WILLIAM MASSEY**

able to seize the German wireless station at Samoa we should feel that this was a great and urgent Imperial service.'[7] This action was, however, fraught with some anxiety. The cruisers of the German Eastern Asiatic Squadron under the command of Admiral Graf Maximilian von Spee were known to be out in the Pacific, and they greatly outgunned any escort that could be provided for the expeditionary force before it sailed from New Zealand. Fortunately, the force was able to link up with two powerful Australian and French cruisers at Noumea before heading westward. The takeover of Western Samoa was accomplished without resistance, but shortly afterwards two cruisers of the Asiatic Squadron appeared briefly at the islands before sailing on to bombard Papeete on the French island of Tahiti. Meanwhile coastal areas of New Zealand were blacked out to limit the danger of a bombardment from the squadron.

Pre-war compulsory military training and the widespread

acceptance that New Zealand should do more than simply secure its own shores meant it was able to dispatch its main expeditionary force much earlier in the First World War than it was to do during the Second. Again there was deep anxiety for Massey and his colleagues because of the continued uncertainty as to the whereabouts of the Eastern Asiatic Squadron. He initially accepted the Admiralty's assurances and permitted the force to sail, only to receive an unpleasant surprise, as his then Minister of Marine later recalled:

'Suddenly I was summoned to Mr. Massey's room. I found him sitting at the head of the Cabinet table, his head on his hands, and great beads of perspiration standing out on his large head. Without a word he pointed to a telegram on the table. It was from the Governor-General of Australia (Sir Ronald Munro Ferguson) and was to this effect: "If your transports have already left advise recall. Am advised German warships probably in New Zealand waters." A wire of recall was at once despatched.'[8]

Faced with further assurances from the Admiralty and pressure from the Governor, Massey later threatened to resign rather than have the expeditionary force sail without stronger protection. The Admiralty was obliged to back down. Somewhat paradoxically, in light of pre-war reservations about the Anglo-Japanese Alliance, the Japanese cruiser *Ibuki* was to be a major part of the additional escort. Thereafter the global conflict only fitfully reached New Zealand waters in the form of German naval raiders, which sank a number of ships directly or through the laying of mines.

Gallipoli

The New Zealand Expeditionary Force joined up with that of Australia, and they were escorted together to Egypt via Aden. Combined as the Australian and New Zealand Army Corps (ANZAC), they were deployed against the Senussi revolt in western Egypt and to protect the Suez Canal from Turkish incursions from Palestine. Following the failure of attempts by the British and French navies to force a passage through the Dardenelles to capture Istanbul, capital of the Ottoman Empire, the ANZACs were sent to the Greek Island of Lemnos with other Allied forces in preparation for landings to secure control of the Gallipoli Peninsula and to facilitate another drive through to Istanbul.

Back home, Massey had faced the challenge of a wartime election at the end of 1914. This time it was the Liberals who made an arrangement with Labour. The Second Ballot Act had been repealed, but agreements were made between the Liberals and Labour over which party would stand candidates in particular seats. Reform actually increased its share of the popular vote, but it was left with the narrowest possible majority of seats. A flurry of electoral challenges and some uncertainty as to whether Tau Henare, MP for Northern Maori, would support the Government meant that Massey's position was not secure until June 1915.

Meanwhile the landings on Gallipoli on 25 April 1915 had provided New Zealand with its first experience of major casualties during the war. Miscalculation in the darkness before dawn meant the ANZACs were landed at the wrong place and found themselves fighting desperately to secure a small beach and the steep hills that dominated it. Subsequent months lengthened the casualty lists as Turkish forces counterattacked and repeated attempts to break out from the restricted beachhead failed.

From early 1915 there was growing pressure in New Zealand for at least the two major parties to form a coalition. The formation of such a government in Britain was widely taken as an example to be followed, and as New Zealand casualties mounted, 'Political infighting sounded more and more like flatulence in church.'[9] Nevertheless, there was a month of haggling over the distribution of places in the Cabinet, with Massey being forced to concede more than his initial ungenerous offer of three seats for the Liberals and six for Reform. Following the breakdown of the talks, the Governor took the initiative in bringing Massey and Ward together again. Finally, on 4 August 1915, a year after the outbreak of war, the formation of a coalition government was announced. Reform and the Liberals were to have six ministers each, with Massey as Prime Minister and Ward as Deputy Prime Minister and Minister of Finance. It was agreed that Cabinet decisions would have to be unanimous. Henceforth Massey would have to ensure that Ward and his Liberal ministers approved of government policies and had in turn to accept policies that sought to mollify the Liberals' working-class urban constituency which faced erosion from Labour. Furthermore, given that Massey was never going to trust Ward to act as Prime Minister while he was overseas, the two were obliged to travel together to imperial gatherings and ultimately the Paris Conference. They were to be away overseas from August 1916 to June 1917, from May to October of 1918, and from December 1918 to August 1919. Each time, James Allen, the Minister of Defence, took over the role of Acting Prime Minister.

The Western Front

In January 1916 all Allied forces were withdrawn from Gallipoli in a retreat that was handled much more skilfully than the original landings. The New Zealand Mounted Rifle Brigade went to Egypt while the New Zealand Division took leave in the United Kingdom. Those 'Enzedders' who found themselves in Dublin at the time joined with troops from other Dominions in fighting to put down the Easter Uprising. The following month the Division was deployed on the Western Front. There they participated in the latter stages of the Battle of the Somme, suffering heavy casualties in a largely successful attack at Flers. Massey's son George was mentioned in despatches after the attack and subsequently received a Distinguished Service Order. Although Gallipoli was to dominate popular perceptions of New Zealand's role in the war, far more New Zealanders were to die in France and Belgium.

In Britain at the end of 1916, Massey was intransigently opposed to suggestions that the Allies should negotiate with the Germans. Before an audience of New Zealand soldiers at the Guildhall in London, he declared that *It was unquestionable that we were winning, but it was vital to put heart, soul, and strength into the keeping up of reinforcements of men and munitions. If we failed in either it would be a blunder worse than a crime, leading to a dragging on of the war and forcing an inconclusive peace.*[10] He maintained that such negotiations should wait until all occupied territory was liberated and the enemy driven beyond the Rhine. *If the Kaiser thinks we are going to make peace on his terms it is another of the Kaiser's many mistakes. Britishers will not forget the peace proposals are made in Germany and distrust them accordingly. The present proposals are an insult to the Empire. We shall carry on until Germany atones her crimes.*[11]

During a visit to New Zealand troops in France at the beginning of November 1916, Massey and Ward attended the

presentation of medals, spoke to several gatherings of soldiers and lunched with Sir Douglas Haig. They also indulged
in some battlefield tourism, observing enemy trenches under
bombardment. It was reported that on 'one occasion the
Germans vigorously shelled the spot where the visitors were
located half an hour previously.' [12] Afterwards they stopped
off at a Royal Flying Corps airfield, where Massey may have
become the first serving head of government to fly in an aircraft: 'Red-faced with the keen wind of fast movement he
came to earth again pleased with his novel experience ...
During the flight he had heard the pilot shouting to him, but
had not heard what he was saying. On returning to mother
earth he asked him what it was all about. "Oh," replied the
pilot, "I was only directing your attention to the fact that I
was flying with my hands off the controls."' [13]

During their long stay overseas in 1916 and 1917, Massey
and Ward also travelled to other parts of the United Kingdom.
Most significantly for the Prime Minister, he made the first
of only two visits to his birthplace of Limavady in Co. Londonderry. He was accorded a great welcome, including a
beautifully illuminated book that praised his achievements
as worthy of an 'Ulster Scot'. Meanwhile and equally appro-
priately, Ward had travelled to Dublin.

Conscription

Undoubtedly a particularly widespread sense of imperial
patriotism and the perception that Britain's interests were
New Zealand's fuelled the high propensity to volunteer.
The relatively small size of local communities also made
'shirkers' more visible and vulnerable to public disfavour.
Then there was an appreciation of the opportunity to travel
to Europe, particularly the British Isles, ancestral home of

the overwhelming majority of young New Zealanders. In March 1917 there was a sadly premature discussion at the Imperial War Conference over plans for demobilisation. New Zealand's representatives were adamant their troops on the Western Front should be given the opportunity to visit the United Kingdom before being repatriated. They claimed that large numbers of the soldiers had requested this and their argument received backing from a surprising quarter; Austen Chamberlain, Secretary of State for India, who had four New Zealand cousins who had all enlisted. He said that 'there would be profound disappointment, both among the soldiers, and among their English friends if they had no chance of seeing the Old Country. It is, after all, almost once in a lifetime of a young fellow who has all his way to make and has nothing but his own exertions to live on.' [14]

Despite the high rate of volunteering, there was official concern that sufficient reinforcements were not available to keep the New Zealand Division up to strength in the battles of attrition on the Western Front. Consequently, pressure for the introduction of conscription increased. It had been foreshadowed in 1915 by legislation making it compulsory for all men between the ages of 17 and 60 to register, and those between 19 and 45 to indicate whether they were prepared to enlist to serve overseas or to undertake necessary civilian work in New Zealand. Despite the threat of a hefty fine, large numbers of New Zealand men, including, it seems, this author's grandfather, a cabinet-maker who was married with three children, failed to register. Only 58 per cent of respondents indicated they were prepared to volunteer to serve overseas, the overwhelming majority of those declining to serve being married. Faced with what seemed inexorable progress towards compulsory service, the labour movement in New Zealand split on the issue, with one wing forming the current New Zealand Labour Party in opposition to conscription and a second wing who supported the move declaring themselves Independent Labour. Some trade unionists served on the Military Service Appeal Boards that considered applications for exemptions, which could be granted on the grounds of public interest, undue hardship or religious conviction. A number of Labour leaders opposed to conscription were sent to jail for sedition when they persisted in denouncing conscription after it became law.

Having rejected making specific occupations exempt by legislation, the government found itself supplying the Boards with certificates recommending exemption on the grounds of public interest in order to keep particular industries running. It was probably not coincidental that those were generally industries, such as waterfront work and coal-mining, which were not only essential but had militant unions that had shown they were ready and able to defy wartime regulations against industrial action in a climate where replacement labour was virtually unobtainable. However, volunteering by experienced workers in coal mines and elsewhere did affect production, so not compelling more to serve was not entirely due to fear of strikes.

Discontent

The uprising in Dublin and the decision by the government to provide exemption certificates for the Catholic Marist Brothers (who were not ordained clergy) led to considerable outrage amongst Protestants. The formation of a Protestant Political Association by the Orange Lodge in July 1917 added fuel to the sectarian fires. The Association, based in Auckland, was led by a remarkably unscrupulous Baptist Minister, the Reverend Howard Elliott.

As throughout the world, the war brought inflation. Attempts to control the increase in the cost of living had limited impact and there was a widespread belief that war profiteers were responsible for rising prices. Labour portrayed these profiteers as the friends of the Government against whom it was reluctant to act. A major group that was experiencing prosperity were New Zealand's farmers, as demand from combatant countries and the removal of some of the more productive agricultural regions of Europe from the market pushed up prices for food and fibre. In New Zealand all exports of wool, dairy products and meat came to be requisitioned by the Department of Imperial Supply under what was termed 'the commandeer'.

Although the prices paid were well above those ruling before the war, they were below those obtainable on the open market. Hence the system operated as a means of keeping down the price of produce sold to the Allies, and overwhelmingly to Britain. Massey and Ward were outraged at the 1918 Imperial Conference to be told that New Zealand mutton and lamb landed for 10d a pound was being sold by the British Government to retailers at 13d a pound and the difference used to partially off-set the high cost of American beef on the open market.[15] Given that it was taken for granted by the New Zealanders that sales of American meat were controlled by the hated 'American Meat Trust', considerable insult was being added to major injury.

New Zealand consumers were more likely to perceive that the country's farmers, disproportionately the friends of the Reform Party, were flourishing at a time when their fellow citizens were being squeezed by the rising cost of living. The cost of food for an average-sized family was officially estimated to have risen by 16.5 per cent in the first year of the war, a massive annual increase by pre-war standards.[16] Having previously argued that *there are economic laws, and you might as well try to interfere with them as interfere with the rotation of the earth*,[17] Massey was obliged in coalition to accept a Cost of Living Act. It established a Board of Trade empowered to control prices. The Liberals also persuaded the Government to accept an equalisation scheme that took some of the additional returns from exported butter to subsidise the price within New Zealand. This did little to recapture Liberal support amongst the country's dairy farmers, and the outcry from that sector did nothing to endear the farmers to consumers. Wage-earners in the United Kingdom might have been amazed at a weekly budget drawn up by the Auckland Carpenters' Union for a family of five in 1918. It included 'four pounds of sirloin steak, one pound of bacon, three pounds of stewing steak, two pounds of chops, and one pound of sausages'.[18]However, the Union, which was putting forward a wage-claim, was more concerned that the cost of the budget had allegedly risen 17 per cent in a year.

More frustrating for Massey himself was the fact that increasing amounts of New Zealand frozen produce, having been purchased by the Imperial Government, could not be exported because of a lack of shipping. Some of this was clearly due to the depredations of German submarines and surface raiders, and later the requirement to ship vast numbers of American troops across the Atlantic quickly. However, it was increasingly evident that the authorities in Britain were restricting sailings to New Zealand and Australia in favour of securing goods from across the Atlantic. In what seemed to be an increasingly desperate struggle to keep Britain and its armies fed, there was an iron logic favouring the purchase of produce from as near to home as possible. Food-miles mattered, and even the voyage from Argentina took half the sailing time of the journey from New Zealand. As the Shipping Controller, Sir Joseph Maclay, told Massey and Ward at the 1918 Imperial Conference, 'we are bringing enormous quantities of meat from the River Plate. We can bring in two cargoes easily as compared with one from New Zealand and Australia, and it has been an absolute necessity to bring the imports from the nearest point.' [19] Worse still, an official from the Ministry of Food declared that while it preferred to buy from Australasia, 'The Minister of Shipping points out that we can get four cargoes from North America in the time we can get one from Australasia.' [20] Faced with rapidly filling cold stores, Massey was exasperated that the wares of neutral states were being favoured over those of the two loyal antipodean Dominions. Both while in Britain and when at home he waged his own public and private paper war with the Shipping Controller in Britain to get more refrigerated vessels to New Zealand. It seems likely he had some success in this, although he remained far from satisfied.

These difficulties with foreign competitors in wartime helped to turn Massey into an ardent advocate of imperial preference, the use of differential tariff barriers to favour trade in goods produced within the Empire itself. He strove to persuade the British Government to pledge itself to the creation of a largely self-sufficient Empire after the war. In London in February 1917, he 'pleaded for the immediate establishment of commercial preference in order to build up the Empire. New Zealand would be the Empire's dairy farm, Canada the granary, and Australia the wool and meat producer'.[21] At a meeting of the Imperial War Cabinet in April, Massey gained acceptance of a resolution that:

The time has arrived when all possible encourage-
ment should be given to the development of Imperial
resources, and especially to making the Empire independent of other countries in respect of food supplies,
raw materials and essential industries. With these objects
in view this Conference expresses itself in favour of:-
    The principle that each part of the Empire, having
due regard to the interests of our Allies, shall give specially favourable treatment and facilities to the produce
and manufactures of other parts of the Empire.[22]

In his reply to the opening address at the 1918 Imperial
Conference Massey reiterated his hope that *we shall be able
to go to work on reconstruction and reorganisation so as, in
time, to make the Empire self-contained and self-supporting
in the provision of food supplies, without depending, as we
have done in the past, upon other countries.*[23]
Paradoxically, and contrary to the belief of many New
Zealanders then and since, the Empire was more in need of
further New Zealand manpower for its armies than for more
of its food and fibre. Following the 1917 Imperial Conference
Massey revealed that the British Government had told him
and Ward that *while they would do their best to get food-
supplies away from New Zealand ... as soon as shipping
was available, it must be clearly understood that men were
wanted more than supplies.*[24] Some pressure came for the
provision of a second New Zealand Division. This proposal
was initially rejected by Cabinet, but from London Massey
persuaded his reluctant colleagues to agree to the formation
of a fourth brigade within the existing Division. The likelihood that Australia would provide another division probably
influenced Massey's decision.

One means by which New Zealand might have circumvented the restrictions placed on its exports by the British Shipping Controller was by acquiring its own ships, something the Australian Government did. Massey indeed considered taking that step. Together with measures such as the Cost of Living Act and the 'butter tax', this indicates how far that former scourge of state control was obliged by wartime conditions to introduce or consider measures that he would have previously branded as 'socialistic'.

The crises of 1917–18

The last two years of the war were to be particularly harrowing for New Zealand, as for so much of the British Empire. The resumption by Germany of unrestricted submarine warfare at the beginning of the year had a further impact on New Zealand's ability to export to Britain. Later in the year the virtual withdrawal of Russia from the war and the defeat of Romania more than offset in the short term the entry of the United States into the conflict. The New Zealand Division enjoyed some success in a number of battles, most notably at Messines, albeit again at the cost of considerable casualties. However, Field-Marshal Douglas Haig's decision to continue

> I was told last night by a reliable man – a man I knew years ago, before he joined the Army – that the New Zealanders (he was one of them) were asked to do the impossible. He said they were sent to Passchendaele, to a swampy locality where it was almost impossible to walk and where they found themselves up against particularly strong wire entanglements which it was impossible for them to cut. They were, he said, simply shot down like rabbits. These are the sort of things that are going to lead to serious trouble.[25]
>
> **WILLIAM MASSEY, 13 JUNE 1918**

the push towards Passchendaele despite the arrival of the autumn rains led in a few weeks to a New Zealand casualty list that exceeded that of the whole Gallipoli Campaign.

The New Zealand Division was committed to the Battle of Passchendaele (Third Ypres) on 4 October 1917, gaining some initial success despite muddy conditions. Believing the Germans were on the verge of giving way, Field-Marshal Haig ordered continued attacks. On 12 October two New Zealand brigades attacked through deep mud and in heavy rain, after an artillery barrage rendered weak and inaccurate by the conditions. They found the German barbed-wire defences intact and were unable to make progress, suffering 2700 casualties, including about 850 dead. This made it the bloodiest day in New Zealand history.

The Division's fourth brigade was subsequently dissolved. Meanwhile the first married men were balloted for service overseas. Although comparatively few were to join the Division before the end of the war, this intrusion into the security of the conjugal household was deeply disturbing in a society where the image of husband as sole bread-winner for wife and family was more deeply engrained than in more industrialised countries where married women were more likely to be in paid employment. Massey shared this perception that the sending of 'breadwinning' husbands and fathers to war was particularly disturbing: *I say now that reasonable provision will be made for those men and their dependants. We appreciate the sacrifices they are making. The sacrifices of the single men are not to be compared to the sacrifices of the married men, who leave their wives and children behind them.*[26]

While in no way condoning the outbreaks of violence that occurred against German-owned businesses in New Zealand, Massey certainly got caught up in the widespread, ugly and unthinking prejudice against Germans. Faced with claims that naturalised Germans were buying up the farms of soldiers fighting overseas, he stated that when it came to Crown land, *Only this morning I refused to allow a transfer to a man with a German name; I knew very little about him, except the name, and I refused a transfer on that account. Such transfers have been refused scores of times, if not hundreds of times.*[27] At the Imperial Conference in 1918 Massey attempted unsuccessfully to get agreement to restrict *the naturalization of citizens of present enemy countries, and also preventing them from being entitled to any form of political rights, or acquiring land or mining privileges.*[28] His justification was remarkably paranoid: *We saw them as waiters in our clubs and our hotels, not only scores, but hundreds of them, I have no doubt, picking up information which was afterwards conveyed back to Berlin.*

The spring and early summer fighting on the Western Front in 1918 brought considerable anxiety in New Zealand as German offensives threatened Allied defeat before large numbers of American troops could be deployed. Following the initial breakthrough, the New Zealand Division marched quickly south to the Somme and played a substantial role in the fighting that stemmed the German advance. There was then some elation as the offensives petered out and a series of victories pushed the German armies back with an unprecedented rapidity.[29] The Division was prominent in the advance, but again suffered high casualties as a war of movement brought the troops out of the relative safety of the trenches. Meanwhile the New Zealand Mounted Rifle Brigade, serving in Palestine and Transjordan, had participated in the series of Allied victories over Turkish forces that obliged Istanbul to seek an armistice. News of similar developments on the fronts with Bulgaria and Austria-Hungary indicated that victory over Germany might not be long delayed.

Partly due to an embarrassing, premature announcement some days earlier, public notification that the Armistice with Germany had been signed was delayed in New Zealand, not being announced officially until 9 am the following day, 12 November 1918. However, Massey claimed that he was aware of some *leakage … because some young men came to his gate about two o'clock in the morning and raised cheers and sang songs*.[30] As elsewhere in the Allied and Associated Powers, the Armistice was celebrated with considerable enthusiasm, with parades prepared in advance in even the smallest of townships as it became evident that victory was approaching. This enthusiasm was greatly dampened, however, by the fact that the outbreak of Spanish influenza in the country virtually coincided with the celebrations.

Having navigated with great difficulty the storms of four years of war, Massey now faced the task of ensuring that New Zealand's human and economic sacrifice would be recognised in the post-war settlement. He already had some typically strong ideas of what should be included.

William Massey at Versailles 1919

II
The Paris Peace Conference

4

New Zealand's Interests

Massey had a variety of aims and claims ready before he left for the Paris Peace Conference and the negotiations that surrounded it. These objectives had been developed largely during wartime, although they generally reflected much longer-term concerns. There had been considerable discussion of what were effectively war aims at the 1917 and 1918 Imperial Conferences and the attitudes adopted there by Massey (and Ward) were to be very evident in Paris. While there was a general coincidence of aims between New Zealand and Britain, there were also differences that reflected the particular interests of a small 'White' Dominion on the other side of the world from London. Occasionally there was even a divergence of interest with Australia.

A strong and united British Empire

A key consideration underlying Massey's approach to the Conference and subsequent statements was a belief that British power, in the form of a united British Empire, had brought about victory. Furthermore, he considered that this power was the only true guarantor of peace and justice in the future. Certainly it was the only guarantor of New Zealand's defence and economic security. Consequently he was wary of any moves at the Peace Conference that could be seen as tending to undermine imperial power and imperial unity He confessed he was *not at all certain what* [US] *President Wilson means by the freedom of the seas ... but we have to see that it does not mean anything that will be a disadvantage to us.*[1] Nor was he impressed by calls for disarmament: *Without the British navy Germany would have dominated the world. That navy was still the most important influence for the world's peace. We must be careful how we allow it to be interfered with.*[2] Such concerns were not limited to Massey. The newspaper of the establishment in Christchurch, having expressed its admiration of Wilson on several occasions, was disturbed to hear that the United States General Navy Board was advocating an American navy as powerful as any in the world. After making a reference to the German Naval Bill that had sparked the Anglo-German naval race, it declared that Britain 'cannot afford to permit even her greatest ally to challenge her naval supremacy'.[3] It solemnly warned 'we have never been very hopeful of President Wilson's "League of Nations" becoming an accomplished fact, still less of its putting an end to war. The prospect will indeed be utterly hopeless if our greatest friend and natural ally is to start off by flinging down a challenge to the British Navy.'

Massey's scepticism – approaching outright hostility – towards the pronouncements of the American President had been evident for some time. Wilson, having won re-election on the slogan 'He kept us out of the war', offered to mediate at the end of 1916. At the opening of a YMCA hall for New Zealand soldiers at Hornchurch during his stay in Britain, Massey expressed his opposition very forcefully: 'he hoped the Wilson peace proposals would be turned down, or the soldiers' hardships would have gone for nought. America ought to be firmly but courteously told that as we have carried on the war without her assistance we shall carry on without it now.'[4] Speaking at Peterborough a month later he was more scathing: 'He thought too much notice had been taken of President Wilson. If the latter had used a more effective weapon than the typewriter in defence of American interests, when American citizens were drowned and property destroyed, we would have had more respect for his opinions now.'[5] The participation of the United States in the war from April 1917, especially in the fighting in the summer and autumn of 1918, softened Massey's approach somewhat. Nevertheless, the New Zealand Prime Minister had strong reservations about some of Wilson's Fourteen Points and was far from enthusiastic about the American President's idealistic view that an international organisation could put an end to war.

Similarly, having become a strong convert to imperial preference during the war, Massey was opposed to any arrangements that might make achieving it more difficult. He was more sanguine than his Australian counterpart regarding fears that Wilson was seeking to eliminate tariffs between states, but that was more because he was confident that such a quest had no hope of succeeding than that he sympathised with it. He was profoundly suspicious of United States business interests and was determined that the large American meat companies should not be allowed to create a bridgehead in New Zealand. Yet there continued to be devotees of British Free Trade even amongst supporters of his Government. One major newspaper that backed the Reform Party was not so keen on the crusade to convince Britain of the necessity for imperial preference: 'We feel bound to say that the idea of

PRESIDENT WILSON'S FOURTEEN POINTS, 8 JANUARY 1918

The program of the world's peace, therefore, is our program; and that
program, the only possible program, as we see it, is this:

I. Open covenants of peace, openly arrived at, after which there shall be
no private international understandings of any kind but diplomacy shall
proceed always frankly and in the public view.

II. Absolute freedom of navigation upon the seas, outside territorial
waters, alike in peace and in war, except as the seas may be closed in
whole or in part by international action for the enforcement of
international covenants.

III. The removal, so far as possible, of all economic barriers and the
establishment of an equality of trade conditions among all the nations
consenting to the peace and associating themselves for its maintenance.

IV. Adequate guarantees given and taken that national armaments will be
reduced to the lowest point consistent with domestic safety.

V. A free, open-minded, and absolutely impartial adjustment of all
colonial claims, based upon a strict observance of the principle that in
determining all such questions of sovereignty the interests of the
populations concerned must have equal weight with the equitable claims
of the government whose title is to be determined.

VI. The evacuation of all Russian territory and such a settlement of all
questions affecting Russia as will secure the best and freest cooperation
of the other nations of the world in obtaining for her an unhampered and
unembarrassed opportunity for the independent determination of her
own political development and national policy and assure her of a
sincere welcome into the society of free nations under institutions of her
own choosing; and, more than a welcome, assistance also of every kind
that she may need and may herself desire. The treatment accorded
Russia by her sister nations in the months to come will be the acid test
of their good will, of their comprehension of her needs as distinguished
from their own interests, and of their intelligent and unselfish sympathy.

VII. Belgium, the whole world will agree, must be evacuated and restored,
without any attempt to limit the sovereignty which she enjoys in common
with all other free nations. No other single act will serve as this will
serve to restore confidence among the nations in the laws which they

have themselves set and determined for the government of their relations with one another. Without this healing act the whole structure and validity of international law is forever impaired.

VIII. All French territory should be freed and the invaded portions restored, and the wrong done to France by Prussia in 1871 in the matter of Alsace-Lorraine, which has unsettled the peace of the world for nearly fifty years, should be righted, in order that peace may once more be made secure in the interest of all.

IX. A readjustment of the frontiers of Italy should be effected along clearly recognizable lines of nationality.

X. The peoples of Austria-Hungary, whose place among the nations we wish to see safeguarded and assured, should be accorded the freest opportunity to autonomous development.

XI. Rumania, Serbia, and Montenegro should be evacuated; occupied territories restored; Serbia accorded free and secure access to the sea; and the relations of the several Balkan states to one another determined by friendly counsel along historically established lines of allegiance and nationality; and international guarantees of the political and economic independence and territorial integrity of the several Balkan states should be entered into.

XII. The Turkish portion of the present Ottoman Empire should be assured a secure sovereignty, but the other nationalities which are now under Turkish rule should be assured an undoubted security of life and an absolutely unmolested opportunity of autonomous development, and the Dardanelles should be permanently opened as a free passage to the ships and commerce of all nations under international guarantees.

XIII. An independent Polish state should be erected which should include the territories inhabited by indisputably Polish populations, which should be assured a free and secure access to the sea, and whose political and economic independence and territorial integrity should be guaranteed by international covenant.

XIV. A general association of nations must be formed under specific covenants for the purpose of affording mutual guarantees of political independence and territorial integrity to great and small states alike.

taxing the food and clothing of the people of England in the name of Imperial unity for our benefit is not a pleasant one.'[6]

Massey certainly hoped that the Paris Peace Conference would see the British Empire delegation continuing to operate as the Imperial War Cabinet had. Indeed, he saw the latter body as constituting the centrepiece of the future constitutional arrangements of the Empire. At the 1918 Imperial Conference he had advocated *representation of the Dominions at the heart of the Empire by, in each case, a resident Minister*. These individuals would meet regularly with the leadership of the British Government in a peacetime version of the Imperial War Cabinet.[7] Thus an underlying aim of Massey's was to use the Peace Conference as a means of perpetuating and consolidating the process of consultation initiated by Lloyd George during the war.

Massey's determination that nothing should be done which might weaken the unity and strength of the British Empire appears to have been reinforced by his adoption of the British Israelite view of the Empire's role in working out God's Plan for the World. Half a century ago the University of Canterbury historian Jim Gardner drew attention to Massey's conversion to this view and dated it to 'around 1917'. The Prime Minister's curious declaration at the Guildhall in London in November 1916 that he 'believed the Empire would last to the end of time, and that London would always be the capital'[8] may well have been an early indication of his adherence. Certainly Massey's adoption of British Israelism seems to have been confirmed by the way the crises of the First World War appeared to be resolved in the Empire's favour against the odds:

I do not know … whether the war affected my outlook

in a way that would never have taken place otherwise, but I have never been able to look at things in the same way since then ... The escapes that we had were most extraordinary. I honestly believe that nothing but a miracle – nothing but an interposition of Divine Providence – saved us in March, 1918 ... I say again that I believe that we were specially protected, not because we were better people than the people in other countries in the world ... But we have been specially protected and preserved for some great purpose ... and I believe that part of that purpose ... it may be a century after this, or longer ... will be to assist in ... bringing about the peace predicted by the prophet – the time when men shall 'beat their swords into ploughshares, and their spears into pruning-hooks,' and men shall not learn the art of war any more.[9]

Germany tamed

Unlike the British Government, which had to take account of the fact that Germany had been a potentially friendly neighbour and a massive market, and hopefully would be again, Massey regarded that country almost exclusively in terms of military danger rather than economic opportunity. In August 1917 he summed up New Zealand's aims in respect of Germany as *to dictate such terms of peace as will ensure the peace of the world for many a long day to come, will provide compensation for injuries inflicted, and a satisfactory guarantee for good conduct in the future.*[10] He firmly believed that Germany should never again be in a position to threaten the British Empire, including New Zealand. In the anxious days of April 1918, when the German offensive threatened an Allied defeat, he suggested that eventuality was more threatening to New Zealand, as *in case of disaster Britain would still remain British, but I am not quite sure that New Zealand would remain under the British flag.*[11] He was therefore a strong advocate of a largely disarmed Germany, with little naval power: *I do not think that the German warships will be left to Germany. It would be an exceedingly foolish thing to do … We know perfectly well from what has been stated recently that Germany is not going to remain satisfied for long. The power of Germany has got to be broken now – and broken effectually – so that she will not again become dangerous for a century, or perhaps centuries, to come.*[12] It is probably not coincidental that he got on well with Georges Clemenceau.

Before leaving for Paris, Massey made it clear that he believed there should be trials for war crimes. Without explicitly agreeing with calls in the New Zealand Parliament for the hanging of Kaiser Wilhelm, he declared, *So far as the Kaiser was concerned, he was sure they were all agreed that he should be punished. He was strongly of that opinion himself. The Kaiser was a criminal and should be made to answer for his crimes.*[13]

Samoa

Massey was particularly determined that Germany's colonial possessions in the Pacific should not be returned to it. Memories of the anxious early months of the war, when the expeditionary forces bound for Samoa and Egypt had seemed potentially at the mercy of German cruisers and a blackout had been imposed on the New Zealand coast, made him all the more determined that Germany should be excluded from

Never again! No more Germans in the Pacific.[14]
WILLIAM MASSEY, 19 JANUARY 1919

the Pacific. *[I]f these islands are allowed to become what may be called pawns in the political game, and are given back at the end of the war ... [it] would mean that naval bases would be established in the Pacific; that wireless stations will be erected; that they will become the headquarters for submarines, and probably the headquarters of airships in some form.*[15]

He went so far as to advocate the exclusion of German merchants: *We should not allow such an unscrupulous rival as Germany to come into the Pacific, for we know that the German trader is unscrupulous as a trader, as the nation is unscrupulous as a nation, and that if he came into the Pacific it would be to prepare for the day when Germany would be able to attack us more successfully from her point of view than she has been able to do up to the present time.*[16]

There was strong support for New Zealand annexation from the Reform press. The *New Zealand Herald* declared that 'the German occupation of Samoa and New Guinea was as menacing to New Zealand and Australia as the annexation of Belgium would have been to Britain and France'.[17]

At the meetings of the War Cabinet and Imperial War Conference in 1917, Massey recognised that Australia shared New Zealand's interest in ensuring that German exclusion from the Pacific should not be bartered away. Some months later he suggested that, while federation was not on the agenda, the two countries should move closer as *here we are in the South Pacific, two nations, one race, one language, one in defence; our interests are the same, our sympathies are the same ... We must act together for the purpose of seeing that [the islands of the Pacific] do not pass under German domination.*[18]

It is unclear when Massey decided that New Zealand itself should take control of Western Samoa, and the looseness of the terminology he habitually used does not help. Even after New Zealand was allocated the mandate for the islands in 1919, he referred to their being *under British control* and *in British hands*. Conversely, as early as February 1917 he declared in a newspaper interview that *New Zealand means to retain Samoa, and I am sure that Australians feel the same in regard to the islands they have occupied.*[19] By July he was referring to Wellington's difficulties at the beginning of the war as *due to the blundering of men who were regarded as great British statesmen in years gone by*. Even then he was sounding a somewhat uncertain note about the Empire's resolve: *though I do not think there is any danger of our possessions in the Pacific going back to the German Empire when the war comes to an end, it is just as well to emphasize our position on every reasonable occasion regarding anything of that sort*. Woodrow Wilson and declarations about 'no annexations' were already casting a shadow over Massey's expectations, and he speculated that some swapping of territory might do the trick, as the *time is past, I am afraid, for Britain to add to her possessions in the Pacific*.[20]

At the Imperial Conference in August 1918 Massey joined with Hughes in rejecting any proposals for the islands occupied by their forces to be returned to Germany, to be taken over by the United States or to be placed under international control. By giving South Africa, Australia and New Zealand the task of arguing at the Peace Conference for the retention of the German territories they had seized, Lloyd George was effectively signalling that Britain was not interested in taking them on itself. However, a few weeks before leaving for Paris, Massey was refusing to be drawn on the question of whether the Government would favour New Zealand or Imperial control.[21] The Auckland newspaper, the *New Zealand Herald*, had no doubt that New Zealand should be entrusted with control over the Western Samoans. Foreshadowing an argument that Massey himself was to deploy at Paris, it repeatedly referred to the fact that Maori and Samoans were both Polynesians: 'New Zealand's claim to Samoa will be greatly strengthened by her scrupulous observance of the Treaty of Waitangi, and the generosity she has always shown to the Maori people, who are akin to the Polynesians she will be called upon to govern in Samoa.'[22]

Massey certainly appears to have been prepared to have Wellington administer Western Samoa, despite his earlier scepticism that such island responsibilities could ever be more than a drain on the New Zealand taxpayer. By 1917 he apparently experienced the same vision of New Zealand's Pacific future vouchsafed to some of his predecessors in office:

> *He agreed thoroughly with the theory put forward by Sir George Grey many years ago – that New Zealand by nature was intended to be the centre of an island federation, the federation to remain part of the British Empire, and to include New Zealand, the Fijian Group, the Samoan Group, Tonga, which was a British protectorate, and the Cook Islands, which were already under our control. It was very doubtful whether this generation would see the consummation of this theory, but he was practically certain that it would come in time ... He only expressed the hope that the time would come sooner than at present seemed apparent.*[23]

Towards the end of the Peace Conference, Massey declared that *New Zealand preferred Britain to take over Samoa. [But] this was impossible.*[24] Yet although he never suggested it publicly, there was a sense in which control of Western Samoa by New Zealand itself rather than Britain would make the Dominion more secure. His scathing reference to former *great British statesmen* who had neglected Australasian (and by extension wider 'British') interests in the Pacific suggested that, like other New Zealand MPs who condemned Britain's failure to secure Western Samoa in 1900, he did not trust London always to do the right thing. Were Britain itself to be given control, there could be the possibility that Samoa might at some later stage be used as a 'pawn' in negotiations involving European issues. He had been emphatic to the British Government that such trade-offs should not happen at any peace conference; indeed he considered, rather too optimistically, that the fate of the German colonies should not be discussed there at all. As Richard Kay has suggested, Massey's realisation that Germany was likely to ask for the return of its colonies in any compromise peace had probably helped make him a particularly strong proponent of fighting on for an overwhelming military victory or 'unconditional surrender'.[25] At the 1918 Imperial War Conference the New Zealand representatives roundly condemned as defeatist a clause in a proposal that the Empire should endeavour to take control of essential raw materials. The clause advocated such a move 'To promote the conclusion of an early peace and to strengthen our hands … in conducting negotiations at the Peace Conference'.[26] Before leaving for Paris, Massey warned *I have been given to understand that we must not take it for granted that we shall be able to retain possession of the Pacific islands without a struggle.*[27]

Nauru

In the case of another German possession, Nauru, north-west of the Solomon Islands and just south of the Equator, Massey had a clear economic motivation for ensuring that it was not returned. Shortly before the war it had become evident that it consisted largely of deposits of phosphate and it was widely appreciated in New Zealand that local farm production could be increased greatly with the application of phosphatic fertiliser. In July 1917 Massey told Parliament, *We must arrange in some way for New Zealand and Australia to be able to utilize the deposits there*[28] and agreed with criticism that the British Government had neglected the Dominions' interest in the deposits before the war. He felt it *would be very urgently required by the Australians and New-Zealanders in years to come. He was thinking of the enormous export that was going on in frozen meat and from the soil, and they must in time to come be replaced or the consequences would be very serious.*[29]

While he saw Australia as a valuable ally against any suggestion that Germany's possessions in the Pacific should return to Berlin's control, Massey was not convinced New Zealand's interests would be protected if Australia and its Prime Minister Billy Hughes were given sole charge of Nauru. Only limited quantities of phosphate were mined before the island was occupied by Australian troops in 1914. Having sacrificed a handful of those troops to years of boredom in the tropical sunshine, the Australian Government believed the island and its resources should be controlled from Canberra. Massey feared this meant New Zealander farmers would be denied access to phosphate at the lowest possible prices and would be obliged to buy superphosphate manufactured from Nauru phosphate in Japan and Australia, as they had done during the war, rather than develop a local superphosphate industry. He pledged himself to seek some arrangement to avoid that happening.

Concern about the issue appears to have been particularly strong in Auckland Province, where farmers had been using phosphatic fertiliser for some time in the more intensively farmed areas. South Island newspapers were surprisingly relaxed in comparison. The *Press* of Christchurch declared 'we confess our own inability to see what difference it would make to us if the desired authority were given to Australia … as long as it is British it cannot matter twopence to either whether the one or the other or Great Britain [sic] takes over the place'.[30]

Other Pacific concerns

Another adjustment of territorial arrangements in the Pacific that Massey had some hopes of achieving concerned the New Hebrides (now Vanuatu). There had been considerable criticism in New Zealand of the Anglo-French condominium in the islands, particularly by Massey's fellow Presbyterians, who supported a significant missionary presence there. The New Hebrides were widely cited as an awful warning against any form of international control for Samoa, as the press warned:

'No penal code was enforced against the New Hebrideans, and even murder was not a legal offence, although to restrain lawlessness the Administration and the joint naval commission made arbitrary arrests for the more violent crimes. No attempt has been made to improve the social life of the native or to instruct the chiefs how to rule their villages. Such moral influence as is exerted in the group comes from the missionaries, and not from the Government, which appears to claim no jurisdiction outside the European population and practically ignores the islands beyond the one on which it has established its headquarters.'[31]

While they scrapped over Nauru, Massey and Hughes were united in their strong reservations regarding Woodrow Wilson's enthusiasm for self-determination, apparently even for 'natives' in former German territories, and his idealistic approach to security. Curbing such moves, certainly as regards the Pacific, was effectively an aim of the antipodean governments. This posed a considerable challenge, given the role the United States had played in achieving victory, Lloyd George's willingness to entertain Wilson's proposals and Canada's sensitivity to anything that might adversely affect its relationship with its neighbour. By September 1918 Massey was even rejecting the idea that Palestine might pass under American control, a proposal he had been prepared to entertain earlier.

There was some concern in New Zealand that any peace settlement should not increase what was widely seen as the long-term threat from Japan. A Dunedin newspaper was mildly critical of the directness with which Billy Hughes opposed the Japanese claim to the German Pacific islands it had occupied, 'Yet Mr Hughes has said bluntly what is in the minds of most people in the southern dominions … Their desire is to develop their countries in accordance with their own ideals, and to be not fettered, in doing so, by such preoccupations as might be excited by the policies of powerful nations with outposts established in close proximity to them.'[32] Sir James Allen, a close associate of Massey and Acting Prime Minister when the latter was in Paris, and probably the most knowledgeable individual in the cabinet regarding foreign affairs, was particularly anxious about the potential for trouble with Japan. In January he wrote to Massey to reemphasise his concerns: 'I cannot too strongly impress upon you, from my point of view, the urgent need to insist upon it that the Japanese shall not be allowed to continue in occupation of the Marshals [sic].'[33]

He was particularly fearful that the Japanese could use Jaluit as a submarine base in a future war, devastating British shipping in the Pacific. Allen saw their determination to hold onto the Marshalls as an 'indication that the Japanese intend to rule the Pacific seas' and cited the United Kingdom's failure to keep Western Samoa from the Germans as a warning. He considered that 'we shall live to regret even more the conditions in the Pacific if we allow the Japanese to remain where they are'.[34]

Reparations

Massey was strongly aware of the financial cost of the war to New Zealand, especially in the form of massively increased debt and the provision of pensions for returned servicemen. He was therefore eager that Germany should be obliged to pay as much as possible towards those liabilities. However, by the end of 1918 he was conscious that the concept of indemnities was out of favour, particularly with the Americans, and simply noted that *if an indemnity was available he thought that New Zealand should get a share of it, in proportion to its war effort and what it had done during the war.*[35] In addition, Massey perceived that Germany's naval disarmament and an expansion of New Zealand's responsibilities in the Pacific could be complementary: *if the German navy is to be divided amongst the Allies I would like to have*

*a handy little cruiser or two to come down to New Zealand
… In view of our position in connection with the South Sea
islands we could very well do with a cruiser for policing the
South Pacific.*[36] Such hopes were to be dashed when German
crews scuttled their ships in Scapa Flow the following year.

There was certainly strong support in New Zealand for
Germany to relieve the Dominion of some of the massive
burden of debt incurred due to the war. The *New Zealand
Herald* maintained 'there need be no hesitation in pressing
the just claims of New Zealand for a return of the money she
has been compelled to spend as her contribution to the overthrow of German militarism'.[37] However, a major Christchurch newspaper repudiated the call by Billy Hughes for large
indemnities, declaring that the Allies should not follow the
German example of 1871 or even expect the cost of the war
effort to be repaid: 'To ask for bags of gold would be to
smudge the fair record of our country, and we are sure that
any person of feeling will recoil from the possibility of it ever
being said that while our dead gave their all, the living got
their money back.'[38]

Turkey, Palestine and Russia

Massey said very little about New Zealand's interests in
the peace negotiations with Germany's allies. However,
one of the claims he was eager to pursue concerned Turkey.
Although the casualties sustained by the Dominion's troops
during the Gallipoli Campaign were far less than those they
suffered on the Western Front, the ANZAC landings had
been the first large-scale fighting for New Zealand forces in
the war and had provided the first shock of heavy casualties.
ANZAC Day had already become a significant commemora-
tion in New Zealand. In 1916 a New Zealand MP suggested

that at the end of the war the British Government should take control of the British (including New Zealand) graves on Gallipoli.

Massey raised this suggestion at the Imperial War Conference of that year and secured agreement that the question would go to any peace conference *with a view to having that part of the Gallipoli Peninsula where our soldiers so conspicuously distinguished themselves, and where so many of our brave boys are buried, placed under the control of the British Government in order that the graves may be properly taken care of, and young trees from Australia and New Zealand planted so that for all time the soil may be sacred to the people of the British race, and especially to the British dominions in the South Pacific.*[39]

With some foresight, if little concern for Muslim sensitivities, Massey declared, *We want to make it what it ought to be – the Mecca of the British citizens from the South Pacific.*[40]

Massey also expressed interest in another part of the Ottoman Empire, Palestine. When an MP remarked that the Jews were interested in it, the Prime Minister declared, *There are many other people interested in Palestine besides the people of the Jewish race. It may be a matter of sentiment, but we are all interested, and we hope to see the right thing done with Palestine; and in this connection I may say I am not at all certain that Palestine will be retained under the control of Britain.*[41] Just over a year later, when Massey participated in a welcome to the Zionist emissary Israel Cohen at Wellington Town Hall, he claimed, *New Zealand has a special interest in the restoration of Palestine because of the part her sons took in its conquest from the Turk, and further he believed that in the developments now taking place in the Holy Land we should see the fulfilment of prophecy – the*

Word of God would come to pass.[42] He was tactful enough to omit to mention that this would entail the conversion of the Jews.

At the 1921 Imperial Conference Massey was more positive about the Arabs of both Mesopotamia and Palestine, after several conversations in Paris with T.E. Lawrence, who he believed *has more influence with them than any other living man to-day ... However, the Arabs are in possession of a good deal of Palestine, and it won't do to remove them forcibly. ... We must stand by the usual constitutional principle, that no British citizen may be dispossessed of his freehold unless required for the purposes of the State, and I think we shall have to be careful how we handle these people. They are a dangerous people undoubtedly, and if suffering from a sense of injustice there is no knowing what they may do.*[43]

Massey said little about the situation in Russia and what the Peace Conference should do about it. However, by the middle of April he was hoping that there would be *a stern face set against Bolshevism.*[44]

Massey thus approached the Paris Peace Conference with a set of aims that encapsulated what he saw as New Zealand's interests. Some of these were focused on concerns that related directly to New Zealand itself; notably the control of Western Samoa, securing a supply of cheap phosphate, receiving a share of any reparations to be extracted from Germany, and protecting the graves of its soldiers on Gallipoli. However, Massey was also strongly concerned to forestall any future German aggression and to secure New Zealand as a British Dominion by ensuring that the Empire, and above all the Royal Navy, would retain its relative power.

5
Negotiations

The Paris Peace Conference was one of the first occasions on which New Zealand was represented separately at an international conference, as opposed to gatherings restricted to the British Empire.[1] However, events in New Zealand held up the arrival of Massey and Ward and limited their participation in pre-Conference discussions between the British Government and representatives of the other Dominions. The nature of British Empire representation was dealt with in their absence, leading to New Zealand being allocated only one full representative (Massey), whereas most of the smaller nations, including most of the Dominions, got two. This outraged Ward and threatened to upset the delicate political situation in New Zealand.

Nor was Massey happy with the procedure followed in the Conference. Two years later he complained, *The trouble at the Peace Conference was that we were split into sections, and each section had its special duties and business to look after, and when we came together at the very last the whole thing was finished up very hurriedly.*[2] Having played a substantial role in the deliberations at Imperial gatherings during the war, Massey seems to have been rather discomforted at finding himself the representative of a relatively small and unimportant country at a much larger gathering in which even the United Kingdom sometimes struggled to get its way. References to New Zealand's level of casualties in the war carried less force when set against the sacrifices of France or Italy rather than those of the other Dominions. Moreover, Woodrow Wilson and the United States wielded a particularly strong influence at the Conference, and their views were frequently at odds with Massey's. The latter was obliged to make his voice heard largely through meetings of the British Empire delegation. Early in the Conference Massey was already comparing it unfavourably with his experience of imperial gatherings: *I think it will work out alright though, to my mind, the methods adopted are most unbusinesslike but the ways of the French and Americans are not the ways to which we have been accustomed.*[3]

> [T]he Plenary Conference in which the representatives were supposed to be given a part has been more or less a farce. Up to the present it has only been convened three times and on each occasion the programme has been cut and dried.[4]
>
> **WILLIAM MASSEY, 26 APRIL 1919**

Delayed arrival

The appearance of the Spanish influenza epidemic in New Zealand, which virtually coincided with the armistice, led to the suspension of sittings of Parliament and a consequent delay in the legislation Massey wanted to see passed before he left for the Peace Conference. There was also a great controversy surrounding claims that the epidemic had reached New Zealand aboard the ship *Niagara* with the Prime Minister and his deputy when they had returned to the country from the Imperial War Cabinet in October. It was further alleged that the leaders had exerted influence on the medical authorities to prevent the ship from being placed in quarantine. Massey therefore moved to establish a Royal Commission to defuse the crisis. As a result of these developments, both Massey and Ward were held up in Wellington and were unable to attend the meetings of the Imperial War Cabinet to discuss the approach to be taken at Paris. New Zealand was not represented at all at those meetings, whereas the premiers of Canada, Australia and Newfoundland were there.

Although it had been accepted by both London and Wellington that New Zealand would, like its fellow Dominions, have a voice in the formulation of the imperial approach to the Peace Conference, it was initially unclear whether it, or any other Dominion, would also be represented separately at the Conference itself. However, Robert Borden of Canada and Billy Hughes of Australia were adamant in the War Cabinet that there should be separate representation for each Dominion, and Lloyd George gave way. Woodrow Wilson proposed that Canada, Australia and South Africa should have two representatives, with only one for New Zealand.[5] He maintained he had 'merely been guided by the desire to remove any cause of jealousy on the part of other smaller states'.[6] Lloyd George agreed that Wilson's proposal was fair, 'but he would not care himself to make that proposal to the Conference.' The wily Welshman clearly preferred that Wilson should bear any opprobrium from the Dominions. Massey, like Borden and Hughes, had assumed Dominions would be separately represented, and there can be little doubt he and Ward would have backed them up had they been in London.

Given the continuation of the Coalition Government, the

question of how many representatives New Zealand would have at Paris was a sensitive one, especially as Ward had complained of the 'injustice, humiliation and indignity' of being excluded from some meetings of the Imperial War Cabinet in 1918. In early November Massey *had no doubt that New Zealand would be asked to send one or two representatives to the Peace Conference.*[7] Walter Long, the British Colonial Secretary, misleadingly gave him to believe in a message on 27 November that both the Prime Minister himself and Ward would have seats.[8] Now, when his request that Ward should be accommodated was rejected by Lloyd George, Massey insisted that the British Prime Minister should reconsider in order to avoid a serious political crisis in New Zealand.

Before Massey and Ward left New Zealand there was some discussion of who else might be taken overseas with them. Massey noted, *he had applications from numbers of gentlemen and also from some ladies who were anxious to act as secretaries and typistes.*[9] More significantly, John Uru, Reform MP for Southern Maori, raised in Parliament 'the question of the Maori race being represented at the Peace Conference' and 'a deputation of Maori Members' apparently saw Massey on the issue.[10] An opposition MP suggested that Sir James Carroll, a Minister in the Liberal Government for two decades, Acting Prime Minister when Ward was in London in 1909 and 1911, and a mentor of Maori in the Liberal Party, should go as well. Uru later raised 'the representation of the Polynesian race' in Question Time. Massey replied that the Imperial authorities had received *many hundreds of applications … by different sections of British citizens and that it had been impossible to comply with them all.*[11] He suggested that Polynesians should be represented at the peace celebrations in Britain instead. It is unclear what Uru meant by remarking 'But that is a jolly trip, is it not?', but Massey responded to his bench-mate that *it would be a very pleasant trip, and it would not entail a great deal of responsibility.*

Maui Pomare could claim descent from a number of Taranaki tribes. Like many Maori leaders of his generation, he was educated at Te Aute College, where scholastic and sporting achievement were emphasised, together with a sense of duty to improve Maoridom. He trained as a doctor in the United States and was appointed Maori Health Officer in 1901. He worked hard to improve sanitation and hygiene in Maori villages. In 1911 he became MP for Western Maori and in 1912, a Minister in the Reform Government. Pomare encouraged Maori to volunteer during the First World War and agreed to the application of conscription to Maori in part of his electorate. In 1923 he became Minister of Health. He was instrumental in the establishment of a Royal Commission in 1926 into the confiscation of land during the New Zealand Wars. He died in 1930.

The opportunity for representation of that kind was a compliment that ought to be paid to the Native races in recognition of their part in the war, especially in the case of the Maoris. It is possible that Uru had envisaged a form of Maori representation with rather greater responsibility. During discussions on Samoa at the Peace Conference, Massey remarked of Dr Maui Pomare, *His great knowledge of the Polynesian races had suggested that he should come to the Peace Conference, and, but for the expense of sending an additional minister from New Zealand, he thought that he would have been a most suitable delegate.*[12] The cost would almost certainly have been for two ministers, as it was most unlikely that the Liberals would have allowed Reform's Pomare to go without their own Sir James Carroll.

The 'Siamese Twins' left Wellington early on 12 December and arrived in London five weeks later. While crossing the Pacific was 'near perfection',[13] the last leg of the voyage, a rapid crossing of the Atlantic, was far from a pleasure trip, certainly for Christina Massey, who found the auxiliary cruiser *Ophir* 'was not suitable for carrying lady passengers' and that 'it was not very comfortable, and the weather was most boisterous. One night Mrs. Massey was thrown out of her stretcher and badly bruised against a rifle rack. After that she was swung in a hammock. ... The storm broke the crockery, and the passengers had to take their meals off table troughs.'[14]

Following the landing of the passengers at Devonport, the official correspondent accompanying them remarked, 'The party had a charming farewell from the good men on the "Ophir", although it must be confessed that we were rather cautious in our response to their song, "Will ye no come back again".' The New Zealand delegation was met at Paddington Station by numerous officials and by New Zealanders resident in London. King George, one of whose sons had died that day, sent Colonel Willoughby as his representative. A guard of honour was drawn up, with representatives from all New Zealand forces, together with the New Zealand band from Sling Camp. Mounted artillerymen accompanied the delegation's motor cars, with the band marching ahead through streets 'crowded with Sunday evening promenaders between Paddington and Savoy'.[15]

Much less pleasant for the New Zealanders was their discovery that while they had been at sea Lloyd George had accepted the proposal from Wilson that New Zealand should have only one representative at the already rather crowded conference table. Following the failure of private approaches to the British Government in London and then in Paris, Massey went public with criticism that New Zealand's sacrifice during the war was not being adequately recognised.[16] He also commented on the call from Hughes for separate representation for each of the Dominions on the proposed

League of Nations, declaring, *if the other dominions asked for representation ... there would be a demand for the same for New Zealand.*[17] During the first meeting of the British Empire delegation (the Imperial War Cabinet under a different name) Ward initially threatened to go home. However, he eventually accepted an offer that he should be New Zealand's representative for the Dominions' slot on the five-member British Empire panel at the Conference, which would be filled by each Dominion in rotation. He was also given the honour of being the first of the Dominion representatives to serve on that panel.

Reform newspapers in New Zealand questioned whether Massey should have put so much effort into mollifying Ward, and the *Otago Daily Times* noted that Dominion membership of the League raised constitutional questions that were supposed to be the subject of an Imperial Conference.[18] The ever-trenchant opponent of the Coalition, *NZ Truth*, declared that 'while Mr. Massey has been suffered as a New Zealand delegate, Sir Joseph Ward has been given a few odd jobs as a sort of hall-porter to what has been called the British panel'.[19]

The New Zealand delegation travelled to Paris late via Boulogne and Amiens, arriving on the night of 21 January. They were housed in the Hotel Majestic, one of the five hotels taken over by the British Government for the duration of the conference. It was the largest of the hotels and acted as a social centre for all the British Empire delegations, including the New Zealanders. It had been 'in pre-war days a favourite with rich Brazilian women on clothes-buying trips'.[20] Margaret MacMillan provides a description of conditions there during the Conference that possibly justifies the otherwise surprising praise that *The Times* of London gave to Massey for enduring the 'drab, monotonous conditions at Paris':[21]

'To protect against spies (French rather than German), the British authorities replaced all the Majestic's staff, even the chefs, with imports from British hotels in the midlands. The food became that of a respectable railway hotel: porridge and eggs and bacon in the mornings, lots of meat and vegetables at lunch and dinner and bad coffee all day'.[22]

On the other hand, that may not have been greatly different from the diet Massey was used to. The New Zealand delegation eventually also acquired office accommodation in the Hotel Perouse. Lack of space at the Majestic meant Christina and Marian Isabel Massey, who had accompanied her parents overseas, were obliged to remain in London for a month, together with Ward's wife, Theresa. A wave of influenza struck both groups in February, with the Wards and Massey's secretary, Frank Thomson, being affected.[23]

The afternoon after his arrival in Paris Massey attended the Supreme Council debate on Russia, which led to the despatch of a mission to Poland and some optimism that Bolshevik representatives would attend a meeting in the somewhat bizarre setting of the island of Prinkipo in the Sea of Marmora.[24] Massey apparently believed those proceedings would be marked by '*a conciliatory spirit*'. The meeting never eventuated.

Both New Zealand delegates were then present at the opening of the Conference, during which the American President set out his vision of a League of Nations that would 'satisfy the universal opinion of mankind' and 'provide a safeguard against war'.[25] Four Commissions were also established to investigate particular questions. Massey was to serve on the 'Responsibility Commission', concerned with dealing with war crimes and war guilt.

Samoa

The first issue of prime importance to New Zealand, the disposal of Germany's colonies, came up early at the Peace Conference. Woodrow Wilson envisaged that all such colonies should become mandates under the League of Nations rather than simply possessions of the powers that occupied them. When ex-President William Howard Taft publicly advocated such a policy, it was attacked by supporters of Massey's Government as 'preposterous … absurd and impracticable'.[26]

Massey joined with Hughes and with Botha of South Africa in rejecting proposals for League of Nations control over the Pacific Islands and South-West Africa. In discussions on the Supreme Council ('The Council of Ten' – Prime Ministers and Foreign Ministers of the 'Big Four' and Japan) on 24 January, it was rapidly decided that the colonies would not be returned to Germany. Lloyd George, who had placed the item on the agenda, expressed support for the annexation of the German territories occupied by Australia, South Africa and New Zealand, but left it to their leaders to argue their cases against control by the League of Nations.

Massey spoke last. Unlike Hughes and Botha he did not specifically call for annexation to the occupying Dominion, preferring instead the ambiguous formulation that *the island* [sic] *should be allowed to remain under British control*. Possibly fearing that the Americans would press for some sort of condominium over Western Samoa, with themselves as one of the powers entrusted with its care, Massey referred to what he saw as the failure of the British-French condominium in the New Hebrides. He argued that his call for annexation was based on the strategic importance of Western Samoa to New Zealand and represented a reward for its sacrifices in wartime. He maintained that 'a confidential plebiscite was taken by the New Zealand administration among the Samoan chiefs and native leaders' and that it revealed 'an overwhelming preference in favour of British rule and condemnation of the Germans'.[27] This information seems to have been given to him before he left New Zealand. When Massey was in London to attend the Imperial Conference in 1918, he had received a letter from Allen commenting on an address given by Western Samoans to their Administrator, Colonel Robert Logan, when he was made a Companion of the Bath. Allen declared that 'The address leaves no room for doubt as to the genuineness of their desire to remain under our flag.'[28] Logan had then reported in December 1918 that the chiefs there were 'unanimous' in their support for British rule.[29] In the circumstances this would have been interpreted as New Zealand rule.

There had been causes for discontent during the war. The diversification of Western Samoa's agricultural production begun by the Germans had been stopped in favour of dependence on copra, and the existing commercial estates were seized and allowed to run down. Taxes were increased to pay for an expanding bureaucracy and recognition of local customs and customary authorities was reduced. However, the most authoritative text dealing with the experience of wartime Western Samoa concludes that a majority of the population did favour continued 'British' rule in late 1918.[30] H J Hiery attributes this to local perceptions that Logan was more open to Samoan influence than the Germans had been. For example, he had bowed to local demands that the largely New Zealand European garrison should not be replaced by New Zealand Maori.

On 27 January Wilson made clear to the Supreme Council that he favoured the application of a system in which the holder of the mandate would be very much under the supervision of the League of Nations, with the eventual goal of self-determination of the inhabitants. In the discussions of the British Empire delegation later that day, Massey argued strongly against Wilson's proposals. He perceived a clear parallel between the latter and the leasehold system in New Zealand, maintaining that both discouraged investment in the land entrusted because both failed to provide security of tenure.

Back at the Supreme Council the following day, Massey weighed in on Wilson's proposals in regard to Western Samoa.[31] He expressed considerable scepticism about the practicality of the League of Nations itself and emphasised the importance of the islands to New Zealand. He somewhat questionably praised New Zealand's administration of the Cook Islands since their annexation in 1901 and its wartime management of Western Samoa. He then gave a glowing account of relations between Europeans and Maori in New Zealand. Somewhat to his surprise, he found the argument that Samoans and Maori were of the same 'race' proved particularly persuasive with his listeners. He then deployed his argument based on the advantages of the freehold over the leasehold, and denied that New Zealand would draw any great economic benefit from annexing Western Samoa. Partially contradicting this last point and rather unwisely, Massey irritated the Princeton professor by comparing New Zealand's situation in relation to Samoa to that of the United States in relation to the lands to its west just after independence. He also compared Wilson's beloved League of Nations to the Holy Alliance after the Congress of Vienna.[32] In the interests of 'keeping history straight', Wilson pointed out that the Holy Alliance sought to advance 'monarchical and arbitrary government', unlike his vision of the League of

Nations. He turned directly to Massey and said that there was 'another power in the Samoan Islands … under the regime of the League of Nations there was little chance any Power would be able to play in Samoa the part played by Germany without attracting the attention of the United States'.[33]

With the three Dominions somewhat isolated and Lloyd George anxious to avoid a major breach with the United States, a member of the Australian delegation produced a compromise in which mandates would be placed in three categories. Those territories occupied by South Africa, Australia and New Zealand were to be in the 'C' category, allowing the mandatory powers to administer them as 'integral portions' of their own states. While Massey joined Hughes in initially opposing this compromise, Lloyd George and the leaders of the other Dominions succeeded in persuading them to concede. Nevertheless, the scene was set for the confrontation described in the Introduction to this book, in which Massey and Hughes defiantly sought cast-iron assurance from the American President that their territories would be allocated to this 'C' category.

> I think by the time this reaches you that Wilson's stock will have gone down considerably.[34]
>
> WILLIAM MASSEY, 13 FEBRUARY 1919

Nauru

On 14 February Massey set out New Zealand's position on Nauru, contradicting any Australian claim to a sole mandate over the island. This led to an acrimonious disagreement with Hughes over several weeks. It was Massey's aim throughout to have the mandate assumed by Britain, possibly with a separate arrangement regarding the exploitation of the phosphate deposits. He set out this approach in a prescient letter to Sir Francis Bell, his friend and the leader of the Reform Party in the Legislative Council: *I am fighting Australia for the control of Nauru and Ocean Island, the two phosphate Islands in the Pacific which are at present in dispute. As a matter of fact I do not think that either Australia or New Zealand will get the Islands but that the British Government will finally obtain control and this will ensure our getting our supplies at a reasonable price.*[35]

In pursuing this aim he had a number of factors in his favour. The British Government also had some interest in securing access to such high-grade phosphate for its own farmers. Moreover, Arthur Balfour, Foreign Secretary and a powerful figure in the British Cabinet, was Chairman of the Pacific Phosphate Company, which owned the Nauru deposits. At the very least this meant there was a greater awareness in that Cabinet of the issues involved. Certainly the company's future would have seemed clearer if the islands were under a British rather than an Australian mandate. Finally, the intransigent and rather aggressive positions adopted by Hughes at the Conference had not endeared him to his British colleagues.

Indeed, the behaviour of Hughes in discussions with Massey and the British Colonial Secretary, Alfred Milner, deepened this antipathy. In April Milner believed he had gained the agreement of both Hughes and Massey to an arrangement by which Britain would take on the mandate while a Joint Commission was established to determine the distribution of the phosphate. In Milner's view, Hughes then reneged on the deal. At a meeting of the British Empire delegation on 5 May, Massey found himself in an argument with Hughes over whether the mandate should go to Britain or Australia. Possibly meaning to make the point that farming was more important to the New Zealand economy than to

Australia's, Massey made the ridiculous statement that Australia had *little agriculture*. Hughes went so far as to threaten not to sign the peace treaty if he did not get his way. Fortunately, his Cabinet was not prepared to support that position.

The following day the Council of Ten gave the mandate to Britain, subject to satisfactory negotiations between the latter and the two Dominions. This stipulation provoked a prolonged bombardment of messages from Hughes and Massey to Milner and Lloyd George, and a number of spats in meetings. It also led to Keith Murdoch, the Australian journalist close to Hughes, wiring a report picked up in New Zealand newspapers, that boosted Hughes's side of the dispute while seeking to embarrass the British Government out of the mandate by attacking the British Phosphate Company and by implication Balfour: 'The allotment of the mandate to the Empire is a temporary solution, and Lord Milner is coming to Paris to bring matters to finality. There is now a strong probability of Mr Lloyd George intervening and Australia getting an unconditional mandate, thus upsetting the British company which during the war bought German shares for £570,000, kept the price of phosphate high throughout the war and now stands to make colossal fortunes.'[36]

Negotiations between members of the British and Australian delegations led to a draft agreement in early June under which Britain would have the mandate, but Britain, New Zealand and Australia would share the administration, with the latter providing an Administrator for the first five years. Australia and Britain were to get equal shares of the phosphate, with a lesser share for New Zealand. At a meeting with Milner and Hughes on 27 June, Massey objected to Australia having sole responsibility to appoint the Administrator, and disputed the shares of the phosphate. Following further 'heated discussion', Hughes agreed that the other parties would be consulted in the administration of Nauru and that 42 per cent shares of the phosphate should go to both Britain and Australia, with 16 per cent for New Zealand. Massey signed the agreement just before he left for New Zealand.

Ward had been excluded from the negotiations between Milner, Massey and Hughes, possibly because he had interests in the New Zealand fertiliser industry. He objected to his exclusion on his return to New Zealand. Whether this was, as Massey termed it, simply a *schoolboy squabble* provoked by Ward's vanity, is unclear. Given the likelihood that a difficult election was imminent in New Zealand, Massey was surely conscious that being able to present himself as the man who secured cheap Nauru phosphate for New Zealand would do no harm whatsoever amongst the farmers back home.

Other Pacific concerns

Both Massey and Hughes conveyed their concern to the British Empire delegation regarding Japanese control of the islands it had seized from Germany north of the Equator. However, they could not mount a strong case against the Japanese being granted a 'C' class mandate for those islands when they themselves had accepted a similar mandate for the islands they had seized south of the Equator. Technically the rule that such mandated territories could not be fortified removed their cause for concern.

Any desire by Massey for New Zealand to assist in the further rearrangement of colonial territories in the Pacific was firmly quashed by the British. Balfour told him that the New Hebrides 'had nothing to do with the Peace Conference' and Lord Milner responded to Massey's proposal that New Zealand might administer Fiji with an assurance that the Dominion would be consulted if it was ever envisaged that the administration of the territory might change.[37] Given the large Indian population in Fiji and reservations about taking over Western Samoa when there were many indentured Chinese labourers there, it is unlikely that Massey's suggestion would have found favour with his Liberal colleagues or with much of the New Zealand population.

Racial equality

Race was also an issue when it came to discussions concerning the Covenant of the League of Nations, which was to form part of the peace treaties. Japan pressed for a declaration of racial equality to be included, something that discomforted most of the Dominions and enraged Billy Hughes. All the Dominions, including New Zealand, sought to limit or exclude non-White immigration, and the Japanese proposal seemed to threaten such policies, especially if an international tribunal was to be established to make enforceable decisions in the event of disputes between states. Back in New Zealand, newspaper editors rallied to the cause. The ever-blunt *New Zealand Herald* declared that 'If Japan presses the point it will be necessary for the Dominion representatives to show equal determination in resisting her. There can be no surrender on this question. The issue is not one of equality, but of race purity and of the maintenance of a higher economic standard against that of a lower ...'[38]

Down in Christchurch the *Press* took a stand on the basis of national sovereignty, pointing out 'that if the League of Nations were able to compel a State to amend its immigration, naturalisation, and franchise laws, there would remain to the State only the shadow of sovereignty – the substance would be gone.'[39]

The *NZ Truth*, a weekly with a vast, largely working-class audience, was surprisingly silent on the Japanese proposal. Perhaps it found itself unable to agree openly with Billy Hughes or Bill Massey, leaders it despised as lackeys of the wealthy capitalists ('plutes') and imperialists. However, it made its feelings clear later in the year when it suspected the Labour Party of being unsound on the issue of racial equality: 'The equality of mankind, the setting on the same plane of black, brown, piebald and yellow with the sensitive white, is all moonshine, Socialistic shibboleths, impossible and impracticable.'[40]

Massey never showed any appreciable enthusiasm for a League of Nations and was anxious that it should have no power to intervene in the internal affairs of New Zealand or any part of the British Empire. Even before the proposal for a clause in the Covenant on racial equality, the New Zealand Prime Minister was leery of where Wilson's idealistic concept might lead. Addressing 2,000 American soldiers in Paris during March, Massey declared, *the war had removed past friction between America and Britain,* but added the hope that *there would be no political interference by either nation in the domestic affairs of the other.*[41]

However, the Canadian Prime Minister, Robert Borden, believed that Massey would have agreed 'without hesitation' to a compromise proposal he put forward. It was Hughes who rejected the compromise and obliged all the British Empire delegation to oppose any racial equality clause. Richard Kay is almost certainly correct in pointing to Massey's anxiety to keep Japan friendly rather than any concern for human rights as the motivation for his moderation.[42] The Prime Minister had always appreciated the assistance the Japanese Navy had provided in escorting the main body of the New Zealand

Expeditionary Force in 1914, when it appeared threatened by von Spee's squadron. He repeatedly said that Japan had 'played the game' in the war, and he was a strong supporter of a continuation of the Anglo-Japanese Alliance in 1921.

Gallipoli

Massey's main aim in relation to Turkey, the securing of British control over the graveyards of Gallipoli with a special role for Australia and New Zealand, was ultimately neither satisfied nor disappointed while he was in Paris. However, he had 'many interviews on the subject with Mr Balfour, Lord Milner, and the drafting experts'[43] and by late April he believed the eventual outcome of the negotiations with Turkey would include such a provision.

War crimes

Massey found himself at odds with the Americans not only over the issue of the disposal of Germany's colonies, but also over the question of prosecutions for war crimes and particularly proposals to try the Kaiser in a criminal court. As a member of the Commission on the Responsibility of the Authors of War and Enforcement of Penalties, Massey maintained the hard line he had promised the New Zealand Parliament that he would take and that he undoubtedly favoured personally. He was appointed Chairman of the Sub-Commission on Criminal Acts and assisted it in

> Neither Britain nor peace-loving nations should allow themselves to be caught with insufficient forces against a possible attack. When we remember German atrocities and the latest treachery at Scapa Flow, we can only say 'Never again!'.[44]
>
> **WILLIAM MASSEY, 2 JULY 1919**

compiling a list of thirty-one acts that should be considered war crimes. The depressing catalogue included: 'Massacre, torture, starvation, deportation, brutal internment of civilians, rape, abduction for enforced prostitution, pillage, wanton destruction of religious and historic buildings and monuments, brutal treatment of merchant, passenger, relief and hospital ships, abuse of the Red Cross and the flags of truce, the use of poisonous gases, explosive bullets, poisoning wells, and ill-treatment of prisoners of war.'[45]

However, neither Massey nor the European powers were able to persuade the Americans or the Japanese to agree to trying the Kaiser or forming an international tribunal to try other alleged war criminals. The two sides on the Commission delivered separate reports. The Council of Four eventually accepted an American compromise that restricted the definition of war crimes to breaches of 'the laws and customs of war', excluding 'violations of the laws of humanity'. It gave the task of trying such breaches to military tribunals. The compromise also made the Kaiser liable to face only a non-criminal charge of 'a supreme offence against international morality and the sanctity of treaties'. Massey, who considered that the much harsher European report most accurately reflected the weight of opinion on the Commission, felt that these decisions undermined its work. He attempted to persuade Lloyd George to get them changed, and the latter did get the Council to drop the explicit statement that the Kaiser was not charged with a criminal offence. He did so despite the fact that Louis Botha and Jan Smuts of South Africa argued in the British Empire delegation against any such widening of the scope for the Kaiser's prosecution, and for a precise list of war criminals to be charged rather than simply the promulgation of a catalogue of war crimes.

Distractions

Massey and Ward were certainly not confined to Paris and Versailles during the five months of the Conference. In March they spent a weekend touring the former battlefields and the areas damaged by the Germans as they retreated. 'They saw the appalling devastation and wanton destruction which Germany had deliberately done to Rheims and scores of villages, while former fair vineyards are grotesque cemeteries,' reported the *Poverty Bay Herald* to its readers back home.[46]

Amongst the more pleasurable distractions the New Zealand delegation found towards the end of the Conference were a number of sporting events. On 16 April Massey and Ward were at Twickenham for a rugby match, Mother Country versus New Zealand Army, witnessed by a large crowd, including thousands of the Dominion's soldiers. The New Zealanders won by nine points to three. On 27 April a New Zealand military crew won a thrilling rowing race on the Seine, beating a United States eight who were 'mostly Yale and Harvard men' by three-quarters of a length.[47] While the regatta had begun in sunshine, the final race 'was rowed in a squall that whipped the swift river into sea-like waves, drenched the oarsmen, and severely tested their endurance'. Massey and Ward hosted the New Zealand crew at functions in the Hotel Majestic alternately over the next two evenings.

In addition, the two delegates made a number of trips across the Channel for official discussions or events. Thus both ministers attended a march of Dominion troops at Buckingham Palace early in May. Unable to leave Paris as early as Ward, Massey was obliged to travel at night by goods train to Boulogne in order to cross to Dover on a destroyer. Two nights later he and Ward returned to Paris in order to witness the presentation of the Allied terms to the German delegation.[48] Later in May Massey and Ward were again in Britain, returning to see the Austrian treaty finalised and presented.[49] In the middle of June Massey spent a week in London discussing the availability of insulated ships for New Zealand trade with the Ministry of Shipping and making the final arrangements for Samoa and Nauru with the Colonial Office. He also visited fourteen blinded New Zealand soldiers at St Dunstan's Hospital.[50]

Massey's attitudes to other leaders at the Conference

The portrayal of Massey as subservient to Billy Hughes is contradicted not only by his resistance to Australia's claim to Nauru, but also by the New Zealand Prime Minister's greater readiness to compromise over mandates and the proposed racial equality clause. Moreover Massey's correspondence reveals a great distrust of 'the Little Digger': *Our friend Hughes is like other politicians with whom I am acquainted; he is very unscrupulous in his methods and requires careful watching.* He later told Allen that Hughes had failed to provide New Zealand with much support.

> **Hughes has been most unreliable and has done practically nothing to assist me in anything where the interests of New Zealand have been concerned.[51]**
>
> **WILLIAM MASSEY, 26 APRIL 1919**

In this same letter to Bell, Massey remarked, *I have got on well with Lloyd George and the other political heads and I have no reason to complain of their treatment of me.*[52] When Lloyd George was deposed as Prime Minister in 1922, Massey went out of his way to convey New Zealand's appreciation of his leadership officially.

On the other hand, Massey never had much time for

Wilson. Besides what Massey saw as the American President's impractical idealism and his belated entry to the war, the New Zealand Prime Minister was very suspicious of the expansion of American economic and political power. It is also possible that he felt patronised by Wilson, the academic who effectively claimed to speak for the 'plain people' of the world. Massey was used to dealing with well-educated and confident people – he had a cabinet full of them – but Wilson's manner seems to have irritated him. In February he expressed *hope that I shall have a better opinion of the American delegates by the time I get back*,[53] but it is very unlikely that this proved to be the case after his difference with Robert Lansing over whether the Kaiser should be prosecuted.

Perhaps unsurprisingly, given their shared attitudes towards Germany and mutual scepticism towards Wilson, Massey remarked, *I get on very well with Clemenceau*. However, rebuffed on the question of the New Hebrides, he felt obliged to conclude, *The French are, in many ways, excellent people but exceedingly difficult to deal with where their own interests are concerned*.[54]

Signing the treaty

Massey was exasperated by the time it took to get the German Government to agree to sign the Versailles Treaty when he, like the other leaders of the Dominions, was anxious to return home. He told the New Zealand parliament that at one stage he had decided to leave without waiting, but *I made up my mind that I was going to sign on behalf of this country, even if I had to wait another month … If it were right – and it was right – for a hundred thousand of the pick of our men to proceed to the other side of the world, and incur hardship and dangers, and difficulty, many of them losing their lives, for the great cause we had taken up, it was right that the signature of the representative of New Zealand should be attached to the treaty.*[55]

With Ward already headed for home, on 28 June Massey signed the Treaty together with representatives of the other Dominions and India, after the Ministers representing Britain and before those of France.[56] His was the seventeenth signature.

6

Reactions to the Peace Treaties

When the Treaty of Versailles was signed, a number of details, such as the amount owing in reparations, were left to be settled later. In addition, the treaties with Austria, Hungary, Bulgaria and Turkey were still to be finalised. Massey returned to New Zealand with significant reservations about what had already been agreed. Yet even his interim view of what had been achieved was to prove unduly rosy. Sir Joseph Ward, while not entirely satisfied with the outcome of the Paris Conference, was more impressed that the measures in the Treaty, especially the creation of the League of Nations, had made a durable peace possible. The New Zealand Labour Party denounced the Treaty from the outset. Newspaper reaction, as revealed in editorials throughout the conference, generally reflected the views of the two main parties. The tone was largely one of some disappointment, with varying degrees of very cautious optimism for the future.

Massey's assessment

As early as 8 May, after the Germans had withdrawn to consider their reply to the document with which their enemies had presented them, Massey was denouncing the Treaty in a press interview: *[T]here were many flaws and defects in the treaty, and too many risky experiments, giving Germany loopholes to evade her responsibilities. The reparation clauses were disappointing and seemed to have been loosened at the last moment. The net around the Kaiser had wide meshes. Evidently the legal view of the sanctity of the heads of States had prevailed. The display of aggressive arrogance of Germany's military caste at Versailles should be regarded as a warning.*[1]

Speaking to the House of Representatives on his return from Paris, it was again clear that Massey was far from happy with the peace settlement. While declaring, *to criticize the treaty adversely … is no part of my business*, he quickly got on to *one or two points … about which I am not satisfied.*[2] Chief amongst these were the controls and reparations imposed on Germany. Massey characterised his statement that he did *not think Germany has been called upon to carry a heavier burden than she deserves* as *using the mildest possible language.* He expressed little faith in what he called *the regeneration of Germany*, by which he clearly meant a moral regeneration, a recognition that it had done wrong and a genuine commitment to make amends. In this regard he concurred with some future historians in maintaining that the German defeat had not been brought home directly enough:

I think the most serious mistake which was made was – it was not made by the Conference, but at the time of the first Armistice – in our not insisting on dictating the terms of peace on German territory. It is very easy to be wise after the event; and the whole world was war-weary and anxious for peace. But I am quite certain that if we had carried on until our troops were on German territory there would have been very little difficulty in getting Germany to agree to the Peace Treaty.

He believed the absence of a full-scale occupation meant Germany was able to put pressure on the victorious powers through a 'go-slow' policy because *people throughout the Empire and the civilized world ... were exceedingly anxious for the Peace Conference to come to an end* and many delegates, like himself, *were heartily tired of it.*

Given the lack of German remorse, Massey was far from sanguine about the long-term outlook for peace. He recognised that Germany's large *industrious, energetic, and hardworking population* made it *a very powerful nation even now*, and he believed that power would soon be magnified by the fact that its factories had not been destroyed when a large proportion of French and Belgian industry had been. He continued to maintain that Germany must suffer some substantial punishment to deter it from further aggression: *I do not think that I am a particularly vindictive individual, and if it rested with me only, and I was quite certain that Germany would not go to war again and was not going to repeat the crimes and offences she committed during four years and a quarter of war, I would say, 'Go, and sin no more.' But I know perfectly well we are not done with Germany.*

> In conclusion it may be said that the chief causes of flaw in the treaty has [sic] been the effort to adjust all sorts of Allied difficulties and differences so as to secure without delay a definite, firm peace with Germany and adequate reparation.[3]
>
> **WILLIAM MASSEY, 8 MAY 1919**

More generally, while he hoped that *the lessons which the nations have learned during the war will prevent a repetition of war for a long time to come*, Massey had no illusions that the First World War had been 'the war to end all wars':

> *I am not one of those who believe we have seen the last of war. I cannot imagine it. I know that while we were sitting at the Conference in Paris there were twenty-two smaller wars going on in different parts of the world; and we know now, or ought to know, that there are hundreds of millions of people to-day who understand no argument but force, and who can only be kept within their own boundaries by the knowledge that they will probably suffer severely, as the Germans suffered severely in the recent war, if they make any attempt to injure their neighbours.*

He expressed *hearty support* for the League of Nations. It could not end war; *But it may, and I hope it will, make wars less frequent, because it sets up a great international tribunal to which disputes are to be referred. Consequently, it is well worthy of our support.* However, the best deterrent to war would be if Britain, France and the United States together dictated peace to other nations: *I know that means keeping up armies and navies; it means force. I am sorry to say it, but, as far as I am able to judge, force cannot be done without. If the League of Nations is going to be a success it must have force behind it. I do not know what form that force should take – that is a question for the naval and military men to answer; but one thing I would call attention to is the necessity of maintaining our Imperial Navy.*

A strong Royal Navy was necessary not just to maintain

peace elsewhere in the world but for New Zealand's security: *I feel more strongly upon it to-day than I ever did, because I have more knowledge, more information as to what other countries are doing, and upon what may possibly happen in the part of the world in which we are located.* It would have been clear to his listeners that he was speaking of Japan, despite his concession that *Japan was perfectly loyal to Britain during the war.* Questioned over Japanese fortification of Jaluit in the Marshall Islands, the Prime Minister conceded, *There will probably be trouble with regard to it one of these days.*

Similarly, Massey considered that condign punishment for Germany could deter unnamed aggressors in future: *I know perfectly well that if we fail in our duty so far as punishment for the crimes committed is concerned there are other nations looking on to-day who only want leaders and who would be quite willing to take the risks Germany took and be guilty of the deeds Germany was guilty of in the hope that they would be successful where Germany failed. We have to do something that will act as a deterrent to those nations of which I am thinking – something that will frighten them; make them understand if they commit a crime against humanity and law and order, so far as nations are concerned, they will be held responsible and punished accordingly.*

Massey again expressed his amazement that members of the 'Big Four' had maintained that heads of state, and specifically the Kaiser, could not be held responsible for criminal acts in a criminal court. Nevertheless, he continued to believe assurances that the Kaiser would be tried for 'a supreme offence against international morality and the sanctity of treaties' and could be interned, possibly on an island. Given that many other Germans were to be tried for criminal offences committed under orders, Massey was convinced that *the right thing has not been done in this connection.*

Massey was also unhappy that Germany had not been obliged to pay an indemnity, and he retained the illusion that it would be required to pay substantial reparations to the Dominions, including New Zealand. While admitting that those responsible for calculating what Germany could pay were having difficulty coming up with a figure, he put forward a guess that New Zealand might receive £10 million over thirty years to assist with pensions for disabled soldiers and the families of those killed. He estimated this would cover less than half the cost. He was later to admit that he also hoped New Zealand's share of reparations would give the Government room to increase spending on the navy.

Of the other treaties still being negotiated with the Central Powers, only the one with Turkey was discussed in Parliament. Again Massey believed he had secured what he had set out to achieve – *to place under British control that part of the Gallipoli Peninsula where many of our men are buried.* He conceded that there was still a chance that the provision might be deleted, but he did not think that was likely.

Liberal reaction

Sir Joseph Ward was highly sceptical that New Zealand would get much, if anything, in the form of what he persisted in calling 'indemnities'. He envisaged that as the work of the Commission assessing Germany's ability to pay dragged out over twelve or fifteen years and as normal trading and financial relationships were restored with Germany, 'it will be found that the world has a very short memory'. During the debate he also expressed strong reservations over New Zealand taking on the mandate for Western Samoa, mainly because of the large role that indentured Chinese labour played in its economy and the threat this could pose to 'White New Zealand'. However, Sir Joseph Ward set himself firmly in the Liberal idealist tradition in foreign policy as he enthused over the League of Nations. Once Germany and Russia were members 'you will have the greatest guarantee for peace that it is possible to provide ... The League of Nations is bound to pursue a definite course in the event of any one of the members of the League attempting to break away and go to war.' Similarly, he pointed to the power to expel a member: 'the mere existence of this power to put a member out will make the country that otherwise might desire to go to war realize more fully the seriousness of such a step'. No state was to be allowed to go to war without first resorting to arbitration and any dispute would be thoroughly investigated: 'Now, if we can get publicity, whether the country that wants to break away from the League and go to war desires this publicity or not – if you can get published the whole going to give the people within that territory the opportunity of knowing what is going on, and this will go a long way towards the prevention of wars.'

Germany had been obliged to recognise the independence of Austria, Czechoslovakia and Poland, and it was impossible to imagine that it would risk its membership of the League by going back on these agreements. Ward noted provisions in the Covenant that might end the private armaments industry, yet seconded Massey's call that nothing must be done to weaken the Royal Navy, not least because the other Great Powers were building up their navies.

Also speaking for the Liberals, Thomas Wilford argued that the League of Nations would have prevented war in 1914 because 'a strong Allied tribunal' would somehow have prevented Austria-Hungary from attacking Serbia simply by ruling that such an attack was unjustified. He was very concerned that the League should not be given any authority to interfere with the laws of any country, particularly those controlling immigration.

Labour's reaction

The leader of the Labour Party, Harry Holland, denounced the Treaty in Parliament. He presented the war as a result of the clash between capitalists seeking to find profitable investments for the vast sums they extracted from the workers in their countries. He maintained that, as constituted in the Treaty, the League of Nations represented a continuation of the exploitative diplomacy that the ruling classes of the Great Powers had previously imposed. Reparations would simply require a flood of German exports that would undercut the industries of New Zealand, and making Germany pay for the continued unjust partial occupation would burden her people rather than the militarists.

Peter Fraser, who was to become Labour's second Prime Minister in 1940, was particularly critical of the denial of self-determination to the Germans of the Saarland, Czechoslovakia, Poland and South Tyrol. Like Massey, he noted that the League had already failed to 'end war': 'But already the League of Nations has told the Poles to stop murdering the Jews, but the Poles have not stopped. Already the League of Nations has told the Poles to stop fighting the Ukrainians, but the Poles have not stopped.'[4] Unless 'labour comes to power in all important countries', there would only be 'armament and piling up of armaments, war upon war, until democracy must wake up and put an end to it finally'.

The determined Labour defence of Germany, in the form

of its 'people', no doubt puzzled and even infuriated their opponents. However, the German Socialist Democratic Party had been the most successful socialist party electorally in 1914 and was regarded as something of a guiding light amongst socialists elsewhere. During the debate Fraser was moved to declare that 'If the Socialists had triumphed in Germany there would have been no war.'

Press reaction

The major Auckland newspaper *New Zealand Herald* maintained its generally critical line towards the Conference. It declared that 'Such distractions as the League of Nations and the menace of Bolshevism carried the congress away from its main purpose, which was to punish and discipline Germany.'[5] Earlier it had been unhappy with the principle established on reparations: 'Undoubtedly reparation for injury will be a first charge, but it will be a surprise and a disappointment if the Congress has agreed to let German payments stop there.'[6] Overall, however, it expressed some satisfaction: 'The Treaty of Peace which has been presented to Germany for her signature may fairly be described as a good one. The terms are not vindictive, but they are severe. They are not punitive, but they are just.'[7]

Dunedin's *Otago Daily Times* drew a similar conclusion: 'The terms which she is called upon to accept are severe, as bare justice demands.'[8] The newspaper had already taken satisfaction in Wilson's original conception of 'the freedom of the seas' having 'received … decent interment'[9] and considered that New Zealand should make the best she could out of the transfer of Germany's Pacific possessions to mandates: 'At the very worst it frees us from the grave menace to the security of Australia and New Zealand that was involved in the existence of German outposts in the Pacific. And it may turn out to be a highly satisfactory arrangement.'[10] It was even prepared to give the League of Nations its chance: 'The practical difficulties that will confront it may be insuperable, but that can only be determined by experience, and, even so, success is as often as not built upon failure.'[11]

The *Press* of Christchurch maintained its moderate tone while agreeing with its fellow newspapers: 'It is the world that has framed the terms of the draft Treaty – the world which, while it sees the severity of the terms, has the strongest reason for feeling that this severity is necessary to strict justice.'[12] However, unlike its counterparts, it had not expressed disappointment when claims that Germany should pay the full cost of the war were dropped: 'the danger of pressing for more than Germany can really afford to pay is that such a course would probably drive her into a condition of absolute and unmitigated Bolshevism, which would make her a peril to the whole world'.[13] It was even prepared to advocate concessions when the Germans sought them: 'On moral grounds the case for moderation, in the sense of leniency, is weak; but on grounds of expediency it may have some weight.'[14]

There was a very different reaction from the pro-Labour press. The organ of the Party itself, the *Maoriland Worker* ran an editorial headed 'War on Earth, Bad Will Among Men' that declared 'the peace now being celebrated has no surety of permanence; it has not abolished war, or the desire for war, or the causes that make war inevitable'.[15] It prescribed education, although it expressed some hope that 'this war, doubtless, will make future wars more difficult, if not impossible'.

The *NZ Truth*, hostile to Reform, increasingly disenchanted with the Liberals and frequently in support of Labour's positions took a more personal approach. Two years after the

Treaty of Versailles was signed, it used the appearance in a Wellington jeweller's display of the pen that Massey had used to sign the Treaty as the occasion for a diatribe against the Prime Minister and the document itself. It lauded the decision of Argentina not to attend the first assembly of the League of Nations at Geneva because, in the words of the *Truth*, they objected that membership would make them 'accomplices of the Versailles Treaty and of the militarist form of the Covenant'. The editorial declared that:

> 'We have little reason to be proud of the part New Zealand played in Paris. It may be that our robust representative had not the knowledge of international law and experience of international affairs possessed by the Argentine statesmen. The plea is a good one, for Mr. Massey knows very little and is merely obedient. That will not, however, exonerate him, for if he had the original bumpkin acumen of his droving cow-punching days, he would have had some acquaintance with natural law. Natural law was outraged at Versailles, and Mr. Massey allowed no principle to stand in the way of the most complete surrender to the wishes of his political masters.' [16]

The editorial was well wide of the mark. To the extent that Massey had been 'obedient' to his 'political masters', by which the *Truth* almost certainly meant his imperial 'masters' in London, he had been so very reluctantly. They had decided to accept a much less punitive peace than Massey believed was principled and were moving to spend far less on the navy than he would have considered wise. International developments over his remaining six years in office would do little to reassure him that what he regarded as the soft peace made at Paris had truly made the world, the British Empire and ultimately New Zealand much safer.

William Massey arrives at 10 Downing Street in 1923

III
The Legacy

7

New Zealand and the World, 1919–25

If Massey was rather unhappy with the outcome of the Peace Conference when he returned in 1919, he had little cause to celebrate an improvement during his remaining years. As Germany and France squared off, as Britain favoured a more generous approach to its recent enemies, as the United States moved away from the Allies while maintaining a major influence on diplomatic developments, as insurrection racked much of the Empire and as problems developed in Western Samoa, Massey was left counting a dwindling number of blessings from the Paris Peace Conference.

Reparations and the continued German threat

The prospect of a share of reparations rapidly faded away. The nearest New Zealand came to receiving any was the payment of 500,000 pounds, which, as Massey hastened to point out, was to cover the cost of New Zealand's early participation in the Rhineland occupation rather than provide reparation.[1] At the 1921 Imperial Conference 1.75 per cent of German reparations due to the British Empire was allocated to New Zealand, and Massey foresaw much of this money being devoted to building up the Royal Navy.[2] However, in January of the following year Massey declared that he *had not been so optimistic about German reparations lately*. In response to an MP's suggestion that New Zealand might give a discount for cash, he said that he would take ten shillings in the pound.[3] The following month he effectively admitted the truth of Ward's assertion in 1919 that the determination of the Allies to extract reparations would wane: 'he [Massey] had a pretty strong opinion that the payments would not last for many years. By this he meant that the peoples to whom the payments were to be made would be willing either to stop the payments or take a great deal less than was arranged in the first instance.'[4] While expressing some sympathy with France when it sought to enforce reparation payments by occupying the Ruhr in 1923, he was obliged to admit, *I do not think any dominion of the Empire, or Britain herself, would care to send an army into Germany for the purpose of enforcing what is due under that reparation of war.*[5]

While sustained by his faith that the British Empire 'would be used as an instrument by Divine Providence to bring about the peace of the world, a peace which he believed would never be broken', in the winter of 1922 Massey was concerned with what had been revealed at the recent conference at Rapallo; *a treaty between Germany and the hordes of Russia*. The people of the small township of Otautau *must consider what it would mean if the science of Germany and the immense amount of military material in Russia in the shape of human beings came together*.[6]

The Washington treaty and disarmament

The pernicious influence of the United States on imperial affairs, as Massey saw it, did not come to an end with the

American decision to stay out of the League of Nations. In 1921 it was clear the United States was determined to end the Anglo-Japanese alliance and to press for the widespread disarmament foreshadowed in Wilson's Fourteen Points. In the lead-up to the international conference organised by the United States in Washington, Massey expressed his firm support for the alliance and insisted that the Royal Navy must remain the most powerful fleet in the world: *We cannot allow ourselves to live on the sufferance of any other nation.*[7]

He welcomed the decision of the recent Imperial Conference to at least postpone any denunciation of the alliance: *It was a decision with which I thoroughly agree. I believe that the peace of the world is much more likely to be secured by a continuance of the Anglo-Japanese Treaty than if we had denounced the treaty and a dissolution of the alliance had taken place … The dissolution of the treaty would undoubtedly be a weakening of the power and prestige of Britain – and when I say 'Britain', whether I state it or not, I mean the British Empire on every occasion.*[8]

However, the outcome of the negotiations in Washington did involve an end to the Anglo-Japanese alliance. It was effectively replaced by three treaties. A Pacific Treaty between the British Empire, United States, Japan and France guaranteed each other's possessions in the area. This was supplemented by a Treaty for the Limitation of Naval Armament, which established a ratio of 5:5:3 between the capital ships of the British Empire, the United States and Japan, while preventing the British or Americans from establishing fortified bases closer to Japan than Singapore and Pearl Harbor respectively. The latter effectively left the Western Powers with no opportunity to enforce the provisions of the third treaty against Japan, which collectively guaranteed China's independence.[9]

The naval treaty, which also involved renunciation of the building of new capital ships for ten years, finally sank Massey's rather forlorn hope that the Royal Navy might maintain a fleet in the Far East capable of confronting Japan. Britain's difficult financial situation had already led its government to rule out the possibility. Attention had shifted to a strategy under which the main imperial battle-fleet would sail from its bases in the Atlantic and the Mediterranean and through the Suez Canal to Singapore in the event that hostilities broke out or were threatened with Japan. Here again Massey perceived the baleful influence of Woodrow Wilson's idealism in the potential threat to the Empire's 'main artery' of the Suez Canal posed by the granting of Egyptian independence in 1922, following considerable agitation for self-determination. At the 1923 Imperial Conference he expressed discomfort with the fact that the Singapore strategy envisaged what was effectively an all-or-nothing naval engagement.

The 'Singapore Strategy' was devised to allow the Royal Navy to protect the British Empire's interests east of the Suez Canal without engaging in a financially crippling and dangerous naval building race with Japan. The main British fleet would remain based in home waters, but would sail to Singapore if a major war threatened in the Far East. Any aggressor would be deterred from striking at Australasia because the arrival of the main fleet would cut it off and a major naval engagement would probably occur in the South China Sea. The strategy failed in 1941–2 because insufficient naval and air power could be deployed to the theatre when the Empire was fighting both Germany and Italy closer to its heart. Japanese land forces captured Singapore in February 1942.

Worse was to come when the defeat of Stanley Baldwin's Conservative Government at the general election of December 1923 brought in a minority Labour Government committed to idealistic views about arbitration, disarmament and the role of the League of Nations that were anathema to Massey. Despite total opposition from New Zealand, the British Government decided to defer any commencement of construction on the dockyard at Singapore that would be necessary to service the main battle fleet. The determination of Prime Minister Ramsay MacDonald to push for compulsory arbitration by the Permanent Court of International Justice at The Hague in all international disputes (the Geneva Protocol) was similarly viewed with consternation in Wellington. It appeared almost certain to reduce Britain's capacity to blockade its enemies and to commit it to take action against those who defied arbitration while depriving it of the means to take that action by promoting disarmament. The defeat of the British Labour Party at the polls in October 1924 brought immense relief, though Massey did not hesitate to launch a broadside against the Protocol when the victorious Conservatives seemed reluctant to kill it entirely.

The League of Nations and imperial unity

At the time of the 1921 Imperial Conference, Massey was, if anything, less persuaded of the value of the League of Nations than he had been two years earlier. In the New Zealand Parliament he invited a fellow MP *to take up the Treaty of Peace and see there the names of nations in the league. I ask him how many of them he would trust in case of trouble.*[10] More picturesquely, he claimed at the Conference, *There is a weaker tail in the League of Nations than in the British [sic] cricket team.*[11] He disputed any claim that the Dominions' separate signing of the Versailles Treaty meant they were 'independent', and voiced strong reservations about separate representation of the Dominions on the League of Nations because of its potential to undermine an all-important imperial unity: *What is the position with regard to special representation of*

*the dominions, supposing that of four dominion representa-
tives on the assembly or league two are found voting one
way and two the other, on the same question? That is possible. What, then, is the good of special representation? It is
a weakness under certain circumstances, and I am not sure
that it is of any use under any conditions.*[12]

He was particularly disturbed by any suggestion that the
Dominions could opt out if the Empire found itself at war.[13] He disliked the term 'conference' for meetings of the leaders of the Empire because it meant *con-sultation and consultation only, but a Cabinet also carries with it the right to recommend some definite course to the Sovereign.*[14] He declared that he was becom-ing pessimistic about the future of the Empire because a *drifting apart* seemed to have begun.[15] He

> If these Conferences – I would like to call them Cabinets – if these Conferences are to be of any great value they must be held regularly and the business must be continuous. There must be no gaps as we have had since we left Paris nearly two years ago.[16]
>
> **WILLIAM MASSEY, 1921**

recognised that when it came to regular meetings, the *dis-tance is the difficulty we are right up against*. His suggestion
that a *fast yacht* could transport ministers around the Empire
rather alarmed Winston Churchill.

He later praised the structure at the Washington Conference, at which Lord Balfour represented the whole British
Empire: *Although in the process of discussion and negotia-
tion the representatives of the dominions had and exercised
the same right of audience as any other delegates, they never
voted separately on behalf of their dominion on any question … I need not say that I prefer the arrangement at Washington.* Massey also successfully resisted paying the share

of the cost of the League initially allocated to New Zealand and complained about the level of salaries it paid. He then rather grudgingly recommended to Parliament to continue funding the organisation for another year *when perhaps we shall be able to get some different recommendations from the British Government.*[17] Sending a delegation to participate in the work of the International Labour Organisation, which was to strive to improve working conditions throughout the world, was rejected on the grounds of cost and because *so far as labour legislation was concerned New Zealand was so far ahead of most other countries that in all probability it would take European countries years to catch up to us.*[18] Early in 1922 he went so far as to suggest, *The Peace Treaty really became null and void, because it was not ratified by the American Legislature.*[19]

It was only just after the Washington Conference, when he seems to have believed at least temporarily that a lasting arrangement between the British Empire, the United States and Japan might have been achieved, that he had some praise for the League: *I look upon the setting-up of a Court of International Justice as the very best thing, without exception, that the League of Nations has done up to the present; and I say that alone justifies its existence.*[20] Yet about an hour later he was again expressing reservations: *the danger from the League of Nations is that it may lead to a false sense of security on the part of some of the countries of the world. There is no power behind it – there is nothing to enforce its decisions.*[21] He looked forward to *a combination of nations led by Britain and America ... which will be able to say to all the other nations of the world that they must keep the peace. It would be a sort of national police for the time being, and I believe that will come.*

Despite the rising tendency within the Empire to criticise France, Massey clearly perceived how vital it was to Britain's security and the whole peace settlement. He disagreed with Smuts's suggestion at the 1921 Imperial Conference that the alliance with Paris should be ended:

> *I think our only chance of enforcing the Treaty is to keep our alliance with France in existence.*
>
> *There is another point of view. Some day or other there may be another European war. I believe there will be, though the wish is not father to the thought. I believe it will be so, though probably not in our time. There is the possibility of French territory passing into the hands of Germany, territory within gun-shot of the shores of Empire … At all events, I think the risk is far too great.*[22]

Ireland

Massey's faith in the great destiny of the British Empire may have been temporarily somewhat disturbed by the outbreak of rebellion in his former homeland of Ireland. Challenged on whether Ireland would be discussed at the Peace Conference, he had declared that land was *satisfied and prosperous*.[23] In the conflict his loyalties were clearly with British forces, although he generally managed to rein in his public comments except for an impassioned denunciation of Eamon de Valera, one of the leaders of the Easter Rising who had escaped execution because of his American birth.[25] The Treaty between the British Government and much of the Irish rebel leadership came as a

> **My earnest advice to you is not to bring coercion to bear on Ulster. Any move in that direction will mean very serious trouble all over the Empire.[24]**
>
> **WILLIAM MASSEY, 11 NOVEMBER 1921**

surprise to him as he travelled to the 1921 Imperial Conference in London. However, he took comfort in the fact that the Irish Free State continued to have the King as its head of state, and that Northern Ireland remained within the Union. In discussions he denounced fellow Dominion Prime Ministers for references to atrocities by British forces in Ireland: *Mr Hughes referred to that statement made by Smuts that he thought that Ireland was a stain upon the Empire ... I ... say this, as one of Irish birth and one who knows Irish history, that the Irish have possessed every privilege that is possessed by the citizens of any other part of the Empire, even by the citizens of London ... Where the stain is I am at a loss to understand, and that is the sort of thing that creates mischief.*[26]

He also suggested that the Imperial Conference should note the opening of the Northern Irish Parliament and refused to be fobbed off by the British Ministers present: *I do not think we have done the right thing in connection with the opening of the Ulster Parliament ... It won't do to give the cold shoulder to a very large number of people who have stood loyally by the British Government in a time of difficulty, and who are likely to be a power in the future, so far as it is possible to judge.*[27]

While in Britain for the next Imperial Conference two years later, Massey made his second and last return visit to Ulster. He basked in the warmth of the welcome from the Unionist community, with the Prime Minister of Northern Ireland, Sir James Craig, being moved to declare publicly that if anything happened to him, he hoped Massey could be persuaded to return and take over the leadership of the province.[28] A final visit to Limavady brought a flood of reminiscences from locals and Massey himself.[29]

Turkey

The examination of New Zealand's claim for special arrangements regarding Gallipoli also proved to be complicated. There had been some cause for satisfaction for Massey when the Treaty of Sèvres was finally agreed with the Turkish Sultanate in August 1920. Unlike the other major Dominions, New Zealand was represented at the signing by Sir George Grahame, the British Plenipotentiary, rather than by a separate envoy. Under Articles 218–220 of the Treaty, full ownership of the graveyards of Allied soldiers was transferred to the British, French and Italian Governments, with Gallipoli being mentioned particularly. The whole 'Zone of the Straits' was placed under international control.

However, the revolt of General Mustafa Kemal ('Atatürk'), the leader of the successful Turkish defence at Gallipoli in 1915, undermined the settlement. His victories against Greek forces in Anatolia meant that Sèvres became a dead letter. Indeed the Turkish advance towards the Straits led to a potential confrontation in September 1922 with a British detachment holding Chanak on the Asiatic shore. As British Prime Minister, Lloyd George favoured sending reinforcements and despatched telegrams to the Prime Ministers of the Dominions seeking contingents to support British forces. Alone amongst the recipients, except for Newfoundland, Massey responded immediately and entirely positively. He and fellow ministers took only a few minutes to decide to offer military forces. Their patriotic mood may have been heightened by the fact that they had just enjoyed a pleasant meal and drinks at Government House. The flood of volunteers reporting to the authorities in the following days was generally under no such influence. In a few days around 13,000 men and 300 women had signified their readiness to serve. Post-war disillusionment, particularly in hard economic times, probably increased the attractions of 'having another go at Johnny Turk', but undoubtedly imperial patriotism ran high as well. Largely on the basis of a cablegram from a London *Times* reporter in Riga, which was reprinted in New Zealand newspapers, Massey also saw the malign hand of Moscow and possibly Berlin behind the crisis.[30]

Fortunately, an agreement between the commanders on the ground in Turkey prevented an outbreak of fighting and effectively renegotiated a large part of the Treaty of Sèvres. Massey maintained that during those negotiations, which had also involved Lord Curzon as Foreign Secretary, the latter had refused to discuss 'giving back' Gallipoli.[31] Under the Treaty of Lausanne, signed in July 1923, with the British Plenipotentiary representing all the Dominions, the transfer of ownership of the graveyards was confirmed, with 'ANZAC' having an entire article (129) devoted to it. Conditions regarding management and visiting were somewhat more restrictive than under Sèvres, but Massey had reason to be satisfied with this outcome at least.

Fiji, Samoa and Nauru

In 1920 Massey had some reason to be grateful that his suggestion that Fiji might come under New Zealand administration had come to nothing. A strike broke out amongst indentured Indian labourers, which eventually led to some violence. Fifty-six soldiers were sent from New Zealand for the protection of the European population, the first peacetime deployment of New Zealand troops.

However, it was the Dominion's new mandate that was to pose more profound problems. Even while the Peace Conference had been under way, it was becoming clear that the assurances of Western Samoan support for New Zealand rule that Massey had received from Colonel Logan, the administrator of the islands, were starting to prove hollow. The overwhelming cause for unrest was the shocking death toll from Spanish influenza and the knowledge that it had been introduced from New Zealand via the vessel *Talune*, which should have been quarantined by the authorities on arrival at Apia but was not. Locals were able to contrast their situation with that in nearby American Samoa, where strict quarantine procedures protected its people. Over 8,500 Western Samoans died, around a fifth of the population.

In late April 1919, as New Zealand's Acting Prime Minister, James Allen informed Massey in a letter that would have arrived late in the Conference that a Samoan petition calling for the replacement of Logan and administration by the United States had gathered considerable support, even though this part of the plea was later withdrawn.[32] The officer then acting as Administrator while Logan was in New Zealand, Colonel Tate, who was 'very tactful with the natives', apparently persuaded the petitioners to withdraw the remainder of the petition as well.

Late in 1919 the right to nominate *faipules* (chiefs) was arrogated by the Administration and all Samoan land was declared to be Crown land. The following year the locally unpopular practice of bringing in Chinese labourers to work on commercial plantations was resumed. The expulsion of Germans from the islands, many of who had Samoan families, also caused considerable disruption. At the end of 1921 several *faipule* sent a petition to the King asking, without success, that the mandate should be transferred from New Zealand to the United Kingdom. In 1922 the new Administrator, Colonel Tate, reintroduced the traditional practice of banishment from villages, but allocated it to the Administrator alone. Tate's successor, Major-General George Richardson, made considerable use of that power and added the authority to remove chiefly titles. By the time of Massey's death in 1925 there was considerable discontent in the new mandate.[33]

Massey was at least able to congratulate himself, however, on securing a share of Nauru's phosphate for New Zealand. By the 1923 general election he was claiming that New Zealand farmers were purchasing the fertiliser for half the price that reigned during the war. Perhaps more importantly, in light of his narrow victory in the next election, he remarked, *Settlers have told me over and over again that the Nauru purchase was the best bargain the Government ever made.*[34]

Immigration and race

Another aspect of the Paris Peace Settlement in which Massey and most of his fellow New Zealanders could take some comfort was its rejection of any moves that might have undermined the Dominion's racially exclusive immigration policy. Indeed, faced with what seemed to be a growing propensity for Chinese and Indian people to come to New Zealand, the Reform Government passed a new Immigration Restriction Act in 1920. This eschewed the traditional technique of requiring prospective immigrants to sit a dictation test in a European language before being permitted entry to the country. It was widely held that such tests simply tested their capacity to memorise what in New Zealand was part of a fixed schedule. There was also an awareness, not least on the part of Massey himself, that Indian troops had played a very significant part in the victory in the First World War and that explicit discrimination against Indians could provoke unrest in an immensely important part of the Empire.

The solution was to introduce a clause that required all individuals not of British or Irish birth or parentage to apply from overseas if they wished to enter New Zealand. The Minister of Customs was empowered to accept or reject such applications without having to give any reason, and there was no provision for appeal. By the beginning of 1922, William Downie Stewart, the Minister, declared the Act to be a success in the light of recent immigration statistics. He considered that it was likely to be copied elsewhere in the Empire 'because it was the most ingenious method of regulating immigration yet devised'.[35] In the case of Chinese immigrants, 'Cabinet fixed the number allowed in [each year] at not more than 100, irrespective of how many went away'. An attempt was being made to reach 'a friendly arrangement with the Chinese Consul' under which thumb-printing might be dropped in return for acceptance that very limited numbers of Chinese arrivals would be approved for entry.

Migration within the Empire, particularly of Indians, was a major topic at the 1921 Imperial Conference. Speaking in front of His Highness the Maharao of Cutch GCSI, GCIE and the Hon. Srinivasa-Sastri, Massey maintained that in the case of New Zealand *[t]he difficulty is an economic difficulty, that is the trouble. The great majority of the Dominion are wage-earners, workers, and they have got their leaders. I am sorry to say there are agitators amongst them who lead them to believe that it means ruin if a few Indian citizens come into the country. I do not believe it for a moment, but I dare say that the legislation of 1920 was absolutely necessary, and I believe it is working satisfactorily; and while facing any difficulties which may occur in the future, I stand by the principle absolutely.*[36]

Back in Wellington, Massey was not inclined to blame

'agitators' for necessitating the legislation. He recalled what had been discussed in 1921 and prefaced his remarks to the New Zealand Parliament with the statement, *I am very strongly of the opinion that we should keep this country a white man's country. I know what may possibly happen.* He then outlined what seemed to be an informal arrangement within the framework of the 1920 Act: *The representatives of the Indian Government … were very good indeed. They agreed to the proposal that is now the law of this country – that Indians should not come here without the consent of the New Zealand Government unless they come for pleasure, for business, or for health reasons, and then they are allowed to stay for six months, and no longer, without any objection being taken. That is practically our law to-day and … my support will go in that direction.*

During 1924 there was concern that the British Labour Government's enthusiasm for compulsory arbitration internationally might make New Zealand's immigration laws the subject of a ruling by an unsympathetic tribunal. Thomas Wilford, Leader of the Liberal Party, quoted a suggestion from the London *Daily Mail* that the Royal Navy might end up being used against Australia and New Zealand to force a change in their immigration policies. Massey declared, *this country was not going to arbitrate as to whether coloured people should or should not be allowed in. They would not come in without our permission, League or no League.*[37] Again, the defeat of the British Labour Government removed the threat.

Imperial preference
Massey continued with his crusade for imperial preference to the end of his life. Together with the Prime Minister of

Australia, Stanley Bruce, he made it a central issue at the Imperial Economic Conference and the Imperial Conference in 1923. The enthusiastic response of so many New Zealanders to the call for volunteers during the Chanak crisis provided him with further ammunition. When the British Conservative Prime Minister, Stanley Baldwin, surprised observers by deciding to call a general election on the issue of the introduction of a very limited degree of imperial preference, Massey effectively entered the election debate on the side of the Government. This was despite the fact that Baldwin's proposals entailed little benefit for New Zealand. As he travelled home across the Atlantic and Canada, it became evident that the British electorate had plumped for continued free trade. Worse than that, the Coalition Government that emerged was led by the Labour Party. Although Massey was to have the satisfaction of seeing that Government defeated before he died two years later, it was clear that imperial preference was off the political agenda in Britain for the foreseeable future.

'It was Mr. Massey who, stamping his feet, asked what was the use of being Prime Minister unless one could be a first-class commercial traveller for his own country.'[38]

JAMES CRAIG, PRIME MINISTER OF NORTHERN IRELAND AND VISCOUNT CRAIGAVON, 6 FEBRUARY 1930

So as he neared the end of his life, international developments since the Peace Conference had not been, on balance, particularly positive from Massey's point of view. True, New Zealand was benefiting from the deal on Nauru; and Western Samoa, while already mildly troublesome, was apparently firmly under Wellington's control. The Irish Treaty had seen most of Ulster's loyalists securely within the United Kingdom, and the Irish Free State was apparently as much a part of the

British Empire as New Zealand itself. The graves on Gallipoli had been made secure.

However, Germany was clearly unrepentant, the prospect of reparations had evaporated and there was a distinct danger that a union of German militarism and Russian Bolshevism might spawn a new war. The Anglo-Japanese alliance, a source of so much comfort early in the war, had ended and had not been replaced with the sort of Anglo-American (or Anglo-American-Japanese) alliance that he thought could police the world. The seeds of imperial preference had fallen on stony ground. Furthermore, there were disturbing signs of waywardness amongst the Dominions and a misguided enthusiasm for disarmament threatened to undermine the power of the Royal Navy, so vital to New Zealand. There was much to trouble the aging statesman, and relatively little comfort to be found in the domestic political scene either.

8
Domestic Politics, 1919–25

Massey's last six years in politics were no more comfortable at home than they were abroad; and although he was able to claim the honour of being the sole wartime leader still in office at the 1923 Imperial Conference, the distinction had its cost. While Reform was returned to power with a large majority in the 1919 election, its share of the vote had plummeted. The subsequent three years were marked by industrial unrest and by the sharp depression of 1921–2. Then the general election at the end of 1922 cut Reform's majority to the bone and left Massey struggling to ensure he could get his Government's programme passed. He only managed with the help of three Liberal or Independent Liberal MPs who would not countenance a Liberal Government dependent on the 'extremist' Labour Party. He found the constant need to ensure he had the numbers on legislation and any issue the Opposition might raise exhausting, particularly as his health was frequently troublesome.

Domestic political considerations impinged on Massey's statesmanship even before the Paris Conference ended. It was clear that Sir Joseph Ward wished to end the Coalition as soon as possible in order to position the Liberal Party for the approaching election. By-election results in 1918 had given the Labour Party thumping victories, and the Liberal Party in particular faced the possibility of having to fight hard to retain its working-class support, especially in the cities. Ward left the Conference before the signing of the Treaty of Versailles, and Massey was obliged to race to catch him up in order to avoid his deputy assuming, at least for a time, the acting premiership in New Zealand. Driven rapidly from the signing ceremony to catch the train to Le Havre, Massey embarked on a Royal Navy destroyer, which intercepted the trans-Atlantic liner *Mauretania* that was carrying Ward and transferred the Prime Minister to it.

A fortnight after returning to New Zealand with Massey, Ward announced he was resigning all his portfolios. Simultaneously he issued a decidedly radical programme for the Liberal Party, clearly designed to protect its left flank from inroads by Labour. The programme included the nationalisation of the Bank of New Zealand, the Cook Strait ferry services, the production of electricity, coal-mining, meat freezing works and flour mills. Vast expenditure was envisaged on public works and land settlement.

As in so many former combatant countries, the first years of peace saw considerable political and industrial upheaval in New Zealand. There were several strikes; trade unions, their power enhanced by labour shortages and continued relative prosperity, sought to improve pay and conditions for their members, as pay in particular was eroded by the continuation of wartime inflation. In 1916, unions in a number of transport industries had formed a Transport Advisory Board and in 1919, miners, seamen and some agricultural workers joined with them to create the Alliance of Labour. To a large extent this was a resurgence of the pre-war 'Red' Federation of Labour in that it rejected the arbitration system, emphasised direct action and included many who looked to achieve the overthrow of capitalism by strikes or even more forceful means. The Communist Revolution in Russia inspired some of the militancy and there was hopelessly optimistic talk of revolution in New Zealand as well. While Massey and Ward were in Europe there were numerous strikes in the coal mines, with issues including demands for nationalisation or worker control. Disputes also occurred on the tramways, in the freezing works, on the waterfront and with railway employees. Coal supplies ran short in New Zealand cities during the winter.

New Zealand has very substantial coal deposits, but most are far from its major port cities. The introduction of railways and steamships was therefore vital to coal-mining's development, providing heavy transport and part of its market during the late nineteenth century. Steam-power was also important in the country's processing and manufacturing industries, as well as domestic heating and cooking. Coal-miners became famous for their industrial and political militancy, confronting the typically large companies that employed them and nurturing a particularly strong class consciousness in what were generally quite isolated communities.

The drive for prohibition also came close to success and engendered fierce political conflict. It had gained additional force during the war, with pledges to abstain from alcohol for the duration, criticism of the wastefulness of the production of liquor during the crisis, the banning of the 'shouting' of drinks and the introduction of six o'clock closing in public bars. The latter curfew, promulgated in 1917 as a temporary measure, was to become a feature of New Zealand life, being supported by a referendum in 1949. It was only overturned by a further referendum in 1967. A poll held in April 1919 gave prohibition a majority initially, but the result was reversed as the votes of the soldiers overseas, which were overwhelmingly for continuance, were taken into account. Nevertheless, the regular liquor poll held at the same time as the general election in December gave prohibition a significant margin over continuance. It was only the fact that the votes for a third option, 'state purchase and control', had to be counted effectively as votes for continuance that prevented New Zealand following the United States into an experiment with prohibition during the 1920s.

Returned servicemen proved less of a source of disorder than had been feared by the authorities, but they were involved in some forceful demonstrations over what was seen as inadequate compensation by the government. On one occasion a mass protest outside Parliament led to an attempt to storm inside. Returned servicemen were also involved in at least one well-organised attack against a Chinese-owned shop; race became a bitter issue with many of them, as it did elsewhere in the Empire. The three main political parties competed in their promises to the returnees, most notably in terms of size of the gratuity the state would give them for length of service.

Meanwhile the Protestant Political Association and the Reverend Howard Elliott maintained a high profile. Having understandably decided that Reform presented the best chance of seeing its programme enacted, Elliott focused on supporting that party's candidates (even one who was a Catholic) in preference to Liberals or Labour. The Association campaigned vigorously and was to take the credit for the defeat of Sir Joseph Ward in his citadel of Awarua in Southland.

The 1919 election campaign itself was fiercely fought, with meetings becoming extremely rowdy. Wartime discontents spilled over, particularly in working-class areas. Taunted by Labour supporters even in his stronghold of rural South Auckland, Massey boomed, *All the 'Red Feds', and 'I.W.W.'s' and Sinn Feiners in New Zealand can't keep me out.* Less attractively he told an interjector with an Irish brogue, '*You go back to Ireland. We don't want you here.*'[2] Christchurch, rapidly moving from 'the Liberal city' to 'the Labour city', gave the Prime Minister a particularly rough reception, not for the first time. A newspaper that supported Reform described his election meeting in the largest hall available, the Colosseum:

> All the 'Red Feds', and 'I.W.W.'s' and Sinn Feiners in New Zealand can't keep me out.[1]
>
> WILLIAM MASSEY, 24 NOVEMBER 1919

'... with men struggling to approach the doors and scores of people ventilating personal grievances or political convictions. ... There was not seating accommodation left for anyone in the building a quarter of an hour before the announced time of opening the meeting and as there was a large percentage of ladies present the exceptionally large posses of police on special duty would not allow any more people to enter ... Just as the Mayor proceeded to open the meeting a determined storm was set up by a section of those who were locked out on a fire escape, and the chairman's remarks were inaudible because a great din was set up by the battering rams of the stormers ... Mr Massey ... had hardly expressed his pleasure at seeing such a huge gathering when his voice was drowned by the excited efforts of the battering rams on the side doors, and these giving way hundreds of men poured into the already overpacked audience like Niagara Falls.'[3]

The meeting was abandoned.

While Reform's share of the vote fell to a mere 37 per cent, Massey emerged from the 1919 general election with the only clear majority in the House of Representatives he was ever to enjoy. His success in large measure reflected the fact that most of the vote for the Opposition was split two ways. Ward's gamble on a radical platform failed, as many of the Liberals' traditional voters shifted to support the Labour Party. Others, deterred by the radicalism and fearful of Labour, may well have shifted to Reform, helping to keep its vote up. The nightmare which the *NZ Truth* had warned against earlier in the year had materialised: 'While it is satisfactory to believe that Labor in New Zealand will replace the Liberal Party, the fact must not be lost sight that Labor will succeed at the expense of the Liberal Party, and that the danger which must be averted at all costs is, that the Reform reactionaries will not regain power at the expense of both Liberal and Labor.'[4]

With Elliott and the Protestant Political Association triumphant, claiming very dubiously the support of well over half the House of Representatives, sectarian issues spilled over into the 1920s. In 1920 a Marriage Amendment Bill was introduced. This was effectively a challenge to the *Ne Temere* decree, making it illegal to say that a legally valid marriage was not a true marriage. It received the support of all Reform MPs, including Massey, and the fierce opposition of Labour and most Liberal MPs. Opponents claimed that this was the pay-off to the PPA for their support in the previous year's election. Many years later a member of the PPA maintained he had acted as an intermediary between Massey and Elliott, but whether the Marriage Amendment Act was involved is less clear. The Chairman of the Canterbury Division of the Reform Party in the 1920s also believed that 'Massey preferred not to accept Catholic candidates. His wishes were known and discreetly followed.'[5] No one was ever prosecuted under the Marriage Amendment Act.

The post war economic buoyancy continued during 1920 and into 1921, with government spending on repatriation, not least the settlement of soldiers on farms, helping to foster activity. However, by the end of 1921 international commodity prices were plunging as the world economy contracted and the commandeer was wound up. New Zealand was hit hard, and Massey's Government moved to retrench as its income from taxation and services dropped. The pay of government employees was cut, leading the Amalgamated Society of Railway Servants to affiliate with the militant Alliance of Labour. Wage cuts by private employers provoked further industrial unrest, with strikes in freezing works and shipping during 1922. Vast sums owed by soldier settlers to the government had to be written off.

Faced with this crisis, it was understandable that many advocated a return to wartime controls, and the Reform Party, despite its championing of free enterprise, was prepared to oblige. The moratorium on the foreclosure of mortgages, introduced in 1914 and only recently lifted, was re-imposed. Early in 1922 Massey accepted the advice of some MPs and of a meeting of delegates from the meat producers of New Zealand and established a Meat Export Control Board, which was given the power to license meat export works, a power previously held by the Government. The Board, dominated by farmers, effectively pooled meat exports, regulated their despatch overseas and negotiated freight rates with the shipping companies. Many dairy farmers pushed for a similar arrangement in their own industry. Just as many meat producers (and Massey himself) suspected that control was necessary to forestall the machinations of the American Meat Trust, dairy farmers tended to believe that they were being deprived of a fair return by the dairy merchants of Tooley Street in London. A Dairy Export Control Board was finally established in 1923 and briefly tried to market the Dominion's butter and cheese on a falling market in 1925.

> We shall have a new Dairy Produce Bill again this session ... It means nothing to me whether it passes into law or not, but if the dairy farmers of this country want legislation they have simply to say so and they will get it.[6]
>
> **WILLIAM MASSEY**

The 1921 treaty that partitioned Ireland between the Irish Free State and Northern Ireland did not prevent the effects of the conflict from again spilling over to New Zealand in the following year. The Catholic Suffragan Bishop of Auckland, James Liston, made a speech in Auckland Town Hall on St Patrick's Day in which he lauded the Easter Rising and Eamon de Valera, expressed a desire for full Irish independence and referred to Irish patriots having been 'murdered by foreign troops'. Reports of the speech in an Auckland newspaper led to considerable public outrage; and, despite his own opposition, Massey was prepared to accept the decision of a majority of his Cabinet that the Bishop should be prosecuted for sedition. An ill-advised approach from the government of the Irish Free State through the British government to drop the prosecution probably hardened his resolve not to intervene. A jury found Liston not guilty, but added a rider to the effect that he had to bear part of the responsibility for the notoriety that had arisen because he had used words that would give offence to a large number of New Zealanders.

The Liberals and Labour approached the election at the

end of 1922 with high hopes. The sharp depression of 1921–2 had led to reductions in government spending and cuts in the pay of public servants. It was Labour that was to gain most from the resulting discontent, capturing eight extra seats to hold 17 in all. After the hearing of election petitions, the Liberals ended up with a reduced muster of 20 seats, while Reform had 38, out of a House of 80. Clearly the balance of power would be held by the five Independents elected, four of them styling themselves Independent Liberal, a measure of how the great party of Seddon was continuing to disintegrate. When Parliament met in February 1923, an Independent was elected Speaker, and three of the Independent Liberals sided with Massey to defeat a no-confidence motion. All three had been pledged to oppose such a motion if the outcome might be a Liberal Government dependent on Labour.

> Never try to carry on a Government with a majority of only two or three; it is hell all the time.[7]
> WILLIAM MASSEY

A major weapon Massey was to wield against the rising tide of militancy and of support for the '*Socialistic Labour Party*' during the early 1920s was the capacity of the state to assist New Zealanders to own their own homes. In 1923 he maintained that it was an amendment he had proposed to the Advances to Settlers Act in 1906 that had led the Liberal Government to introduce the Advances to Workers Act, which provided loans to town-dwellers to pay for the construction of their own houses.[8] Now he proposed that the government should advance 95 per cent of the cost of both the house and the land on which it was to be built. He made a direct connection between home ownership and the moderation of political extremism: *There is another reason why I favour the principle of making every man his own landlord: It is that a man is much less likely to take up Bolshevistic ideas if he owns a house than if he is paying a big rent for one, and I know that the Bolshevism which is spreading about the country by way of propaganda is doing a great deal more harm than many people imagine.*

At one stage during the struggle to maintain his Government's majority in Parliament after the election of 1922, Massey was moved to declare, *I won't have members going to bed merely because they are ill. If they want to die, they must die in the House!*[9] By the end of March 1925 it was evident that the Prime Minister himself was seriously ill. An operation in April proved unsuccessful, and he died on 10 May at his own house in Wellington. Parliament was not sitting at the time.

The remark that 'all political careers end in failure', attributed to Enoch Powell, would appear to be particularly applicable to the last years of Massey's life. Internationally there were strong signs that his dream of an eternally powerful and united British Empire was fading. Domestically he was struggling to maintain his hold on power with a small and somewhat uncertain majority. Yet the following year his real successor, the comparatively youthful Joseph Gordon Coates, who became Prime Minister following a brief caretaking by Sir Francis Dillon Bell, led the Reform Party to a landslide victory. While the Party's campaign was heavily focused on Coates and was regarded as marking the introduction of American techniques of political advertising to New Zealand, historians have given much of the credit to Massey and the policies he put in place in the early 1920s.

9
Legacy

Ninety years after Massey went to Versailles, there is little public awareness of the Paris Peace Conference in New Zealand. The First World War is recalled each year on ANZAC Day (25 April) and books on the experience of New Zealand forces during that war are bestsellers. As in the fellow former Dominions of Australia and Canada, there is a widespread acceptance that the nation 'found its identity' or began to 'find its identity' in that conflict. While the slopes of Gallipoli and to a lesser extent the fields around Ypres are places of pilgrimage for young New Zealanders, the halls of Versailles are generally not. To the extent that there is an awareness of the Versailles Treaty, it lies in a vague belief that the settlement was unjust to Germany and contributed to the rise of the Nazis.

Yet the negotiations leading up to the signing of the Treaty of Versailles and the signing itself represent the first appearance of New Zealand on the international stage in its own right rather than as a subordinate part of the British Empire. Massey himself emphasised this point on his return from Paris: *Certainly the signing of the Peace Treaty and the part the dominions took in the Conference was the most important event in their history. What has taken place has proved that their status is assured. They have ceased to be dependencies of the Empire. They have become partners – partners with all the duties, responsibilities, and privileges that belong to a partnership.*[1]

He preferred not to see this process as in any sense a breaking away from Britain, but rather as a strengthening of imperial ties. Indeed, even if the future behaviour of some other Dominions would have disappointed Massey, he might have found some comfort in the fact that New Zealand, even during an idealistic excursion in the late 1930s, continued to see its security, economic and political interests closely aligned with those of the United Kingdom until 'Mother left home' or, rather, decided that her primary interests were closer to home.

ANZAC Day (25 April), the anniversary of the Gallipoli landing, has been commemorated in Australia and New Zealand each year since 1915. Although Remembrance Day (11 November) was initially widely observed, it was ANZAC Day that became the dominant antipodean memorial date. Services were held in even very small rural communities, typically before the war memorials erected throughout the country in the immediate post-war years. ANZAC Day became a public holiday in New Zealand in 1920. Although no ANZACs survive and the ranks of Second World War veterans are thinning rapidly, the dawn service remains a major national event in both countries (albeit with a surprising lack of mutual recognition). In recent years the media have commented on increased turnout at services, with many young people attending.

Samoa

Massey's securing of the mandate for Western Samoa was in the long run to have a profound impact on the future of New Zealand society. In the medium term, however, the consequences were to be unfortunate for both the local population and for New Zealand. By the mid-1920s the administration had come into conflict with both local merchants and tribal leaders. O F Nelson, a wealthy trader and local chief, launched a movement called the Mau, which came to include a majority of the Samoan population. Following the organisation of a Mau police force and extensive passive resistance, Nelson was arrested and exiled to New Zealand. In December 1929 attempts to arrest members of the Mau taking part in a procession to welcome him home led to shooting by New Zealand police that left eleven Samoans and one policeman dead.

After the Second World War, responsibility for the League of Nations mandates was transferred to the United Nations. Independence 'in free association with New Zealand' was granted in 1962. Beginning in the 1960s, large numbers of Samoans travelled to New Zealand to find employment, particularly in the manufacturing industries of Auckland. They and their descendants now make up a significant proportion of the New Zealand population and are disproportionately represented in the nation's rugby team, the All Blacks. In 2006 there were 130,000 Samoans in New Zealand, compared with 179,000 in Western Samoa.

Nauru

New Zealand farming undoubtedly benefited for many decades from the assurance of supplies of phosphate from Nauru. This assisted the development of a local superphosphate industry, and superphosphate became a major element in what has been termed 'the grasslands revolution' in New Zealand. Put simply, the addition of phosphate to pastures promoted the growth of clover, which in turn harboured organisms that fixed nitrogen from the air. The nitrogen then fostered the growth of palatable and highly productive exotic grasses, particularly ryegrass. The combination of such grasses and clover underwrote a massive increase in pastoral production. Initially the growth was concentrated in the dairy industry on flatter parts of the country, where fertiliser could be more cheaply spread from horse-drawn or occasionally tractor-towed vehicles. Top-dressing of steeper slopes tended to have to be done by hand and was therefore often prohibitively expensive. However, after the Second World War phosphatic fertiliser was increasingly spread on hill country farms as aircraft produced during the war and pilots trained for service in Europe and the Pacific were deployed on 'aerial topdressing'. Numbers of sheep and beef cattle in the Dominion rose dramatically, as did exports of meat. Exhaustion of the phosphate deposits on Nauru eventually necessitated moving to other sources, but for much of the 20th century New Zealand farmers had reason to be thankful for Massey's work at Versailles.

New Zealand's appeasement of Germany

A major legacy of the treaties for the New Zealand Labour Party and many on the left and later the right of politics was the perception that Versailles had been unfair to Germany, and that that country had grievances which needed to be addressed. When New Zealand's first Labour Government was elected in 1935, government criticism of German rearmament and Adolf Hitler's aggressive policies towards his neighbours was muted.

Speaking at the Imperial Conference in London in 1937, the Labour Prime Minister Michael Joseph Savage made plain that the statesmen at the Paris Peace Conference bore most of the responsibility for Germany's attitude:

'[T]he evils from which the world is at the present time suffering are, in our opinion, due almost entirely to a faulty peace; that the nations which are now most threatening in their attitude have had undoubted and legitimate grievances, and that a proper atmosphere for the international co-operation that we all so heartily desire can, we think, never be achieved until an attempt has been made to consider and to rectify, in so far as they can be rectified, the injustices of the past.'[2]

This perception contributed to the remarkably conciliatory line towards Nazi Germany, contrasting sharply with the same Government's criticism of Italy and Japan's aggressive policies.

International organisations and peace

Despite Massey's deep scepticism that Woodrow Wilson's 'toy' would ever amount to much, New Zealand was a foundation member of the League of Nations. Massey's sceptical attitude was to a large extent echoed in the approaches of the subsequent non-Labour governments to 1935. The basis of New Zealand's defence against a hostile major power continued to be the Royal Navy and its capacity to use the Singapore Base. No plans were made to deploy local forces in support of the League of Nations in the event of its calling for such support against an aggressor. However, when the League, with the support of Britain, decided that economic sanctions should be imposed on Italy in response to its invasion of Abyssinia, New Zealand complied.

The New Zealand Labour Party continued to attack the League of Nations during the 1920s. However, it gradually came to see the organisation as the best hope for peace in the world, even when Japan, Germany and Italy had all left it, joining the United States on the outside. Particularly during the late 1930s, the League was to become a stage on which the then Labour Government was to raise New Zealand's profile by lecturing the western Powers on their duty to condemn more strongly Italian aggression against Abyssinia, Japanese aggression against China, and the military revolt in Spain. Yet the same government was critical of British and French rearmament. In Labour's view support for the League became the alternative to rearmament, not just for New Zealand, but for the rest of the world as well.

This attitude led it to resist any large-scale rearmament for some years, and then to participate in it without enthusiasm. In particular, it rejected the development of an expeditionary force that might be used in furthering imperial interests and that might suffer the level of casualties experienced at Gallipoli and on the Western Front. While expressing discontent that Britain and France were not denouncing aggression in Europe, Africa and the Far East more vigorously, no plans were made to send New Zealand troops to help defeat an aggressor if a major war resulted. The emphasis was placed on building up a local air force to defend New Zealand itself and its approaches from the north. Consequently it was not until well into 1940 that an expeditionary force sailed from New Zealand.

The belief that an international organisation might ensure peace, a belief that gained extra currency with the creation of the League of Nations as part of the Versailles settlement, remained an article of faith with Labour despite the League's failure. However, Savage's successor as New Zealand Prime Minister, Peter Fraser, was far too hard-headed to believe that condemnation by 'the people of the world' would forestall aggression. He pushed strongly at the San Francisco Conference in 1945 for the United Nations to be given greater authority than the League and for it to be easier for it to deploy military force against an aggressor. Together with the Minister of External Affairs in the Australian Labour Government, Dr H V Evatt, he unsuccessfully opposed the introduction of a veto for the four Permanent Members of the Security Council. Subsequent Labour Governments, and to a lesser extent their National counterparts, placed a good deal of emphasis on the role of the United Nations in New Zealand foreign policy. New Zealand became a significant contributor to UN peacekeeping and peace monitoring. In 2003 it was to give the lack of approval by the Security Council as the reason for not participating alongside the United States, the United Kingdom and Australia in the invasion of Iraq.

Some of the diplomats at the Paris Peace Conference certainly looked on Massey as ignorant, stubborn and uneducated, a jingoistic 'Farmer Bill' from the ends of the Earth, who could not appreciate the fine ideals being built into the new international order, particularly by Woodrow Wilson. Yet in view of what was to happen in the 1930s, it is difficult not to see the sense in much of what Massey had to say. He would have been horrified by the level of disarmament accepted as safe by the British Government until the mid-1930s. He appreciated that the rules of the League of Nations and its lack of military power could never provide protection from another major war.

While he could not have predicted that the Great Depression would bring Hitler and the Nazis to power, he recognised that there were forces in Germany that sought to reverse the defeat of 1918. When the draft treaty was presented to the German plenipotentiaries early in May 1919, he perceived *the greatest weakness* to be: *The proposal that the Allies should occupy districts west of the Rhine for fifteen years does not give France the measure of permanent security desired. What will happen after the fifteen years, even if the conditions have been complied with? There is a very prevalent opinion in France that Germany will come again, though not in the present generation, and military experts urge that the only way to make France safe is to give her the defensive control of the west bank of the Rhine.*[3]

In 1930 all Allied forces were withdrawn early from the Rhineland in recognition that Germany had apparently been meeting most of her commitments. Six years later Hitler was able to send troops into what was still supposed to be a demilitarised zone on both sides of the Rhine. That allowed him to develop the defences in the west to enable him to expand German power eastwards, eventually forcing Britain and France to confront him or accept his dominance of Europe. Perhaps 'Farmer Bill' saw more clearly the best way to give peace a long-term chance than some of his more sophisticated critics at the Paris Peace Conference.

Notes

Introduction

1. D Lloyd George, *The Truth about the Peace Treaties* (Victor Gollancz, London: 1938) p 542.
2. *Press*, 4 November 1918, p 6.
3. *New Zealand Herald*, 15 January 1919, p 6.
4. *Otago Daily Times*, 9 May 1919, p 4.
5. M MacMillan, *Peacemakers: The Paris Conference of 1919 and Its Attempt to End War* (John Murray, London: 2001), hereafter MacMillan, *Peacemakers*, p 56.
6. MacMillan, *Peacemakers*, p 113.
7. MacMillan, *Peacemakers*, p 111.
8. MacMillan, *Peacemakers*, p 114.
9. MacMillan, *Peacemakers*, p 328.
10. R G H Kay, 'In Pursuit of Victory: British-New Zealand Relations during the First World War' (University of Otago PhD Thesis, 2001), hereafter Kay, 'In Pursuit of Victory'.
11. M Bassett, *Sir Joseph Ward: A Political Biography* (Auckland University Press, Auckland: 1993), hereafter *Sir Joseph Ward*, pp 242–43.

12. W J Gardner, 'The Rise of W.F. Massey, 1891–1912', *Political Science* (1961), hereafter Gardner, 'Rise of Massey', pp 3–30.

13. W J Gardner, *William Massey* (A.H. and A.W. Reed, Wellington: 1969).

14. H J Constable, *From Ploughboy to Premier* (John Marlowe Savage and Co., London: 1925).

15. G H Scholefield, *The Right Honourable William Ferguson Massey, M.P., P.C., Prime Minister of New Zealand, 1912–1925 : A Personal Biography* (Tombs, Wellington: 1925) hereafter Scholefield, *Massey*.

1: New Zealand to 1914

1. *New Zealand Parliamentary Debates* (hereafter *NZPD*), Vol.83, 20 July 1894, p 658.

2. W H Oliver, 'Social Policy in New Zealand: An Historical View', *New Zealand Today*, Vol.1, *The Royal Commission on Social Policy April Report* (The Commission, 1988) especially pp 3–18.

2: Massey's Life to 1914

1. At the 1921 Imperial Conference Massey remarked *a number of my relatives are American citizens*. Imperial Conference 1921, *Notes of Meetings (Nos. E1 to E84)*, (HM Stationery Office, London E20: 1921) p 11.

2. *NZPD*, 203, 17 July 1924, p 594.

3. Scholefield, *Massey*, pp 2–4.

4. *NZPD*, 193, 15 December 1921, p 82. See also *NZPD*, 200, 29 June 1923, p 475.

5. *NZPD*, 200, 27 June 1923, p 365.

6. *Poverty Bay Herald*, 6 May 1908, p 5.

7. *NZPD*, 197, 3 October 1922, p 510.

8. G W Rice, 'How Irish Was New Zealand's Ulster-Born Prime Minister Bill Massey?' in Brad Patterson (ed), *Ulster-New Zealand Migration and Cultural Transfers* (Four Courts Press, Dublin: 2006) hereafter Patterson, *Ulster–New Zealand Migration*, pp 241–54, p 250.

9. *Observer*, 25 November 1893, p 3.

10. *Observer*, 5 December 1896, p 7.

11. *New Zealand Herald*, 3 November 1896, p 3.

12. Gardner, 'Rise of Massey', p 12.

13. *NZPD*, 199, 15 February 1923, p 246.

14. *NZPD*, 193, 15 December 1921, p 51.

15. *NZPD*, Vol.137, 4 September 1906, p 332.

16. *NZPD*, 199, 17 February 1923, p 357.

17. *NZPD*, 204, 25 September 1924, p 1220.

18. Scholefield, *Massey*, p 19.

19. *Hawera and Normanby Star*, 6 May 1907, p 5.

20. *Wanganui Herald*, 30 April 1908, p 7.

21. Massey to Fisher, 8 June 1910, Fisher Family Papers, MS Papers 0103–05, Alexander Turnbull Library.

22. *Taranaki Herald*, 6 May 1908, p 5.

23. *Spectator*, quoted in *Bush Advocate*, 1 May 1905, p 4.

24. *Grey River Argus*, 20 March 1914, p 2.

3: New Zealand's Great War

1. Quoted in A Macdonald, 'An Awkward Salient: New Zealand Infantry on the Somme, 15 September 1916', in John Crawford and Ian McGibbon (eds), *New Zealand's Great War: New Zealand, the Allies and the First World War* (Exisle Publishing, Auckland: 2007) hereafter Crawford and McGibbon, *New Zealand's Great War*, p 246.

2. *Grey River Argus*, 12 June 1918, p 3.

3. B Farland, *Farmer Bill: William Ferguson Massey and the Reform Party* (First Edition Publishers, Wellington: 2008) pp 335–36.

4. *NZPD*, 180, 13 September 1917, p 134.

5. *Grey River Argus*, 3 August 1914, p 5.

6. Scholefield, *Massey*, p 24.

7. W D Stewart, *The Right Honourable Sir Francis H.D. Bell, P.C., G.C.M.G., K.C., His Life and Times* (Butterworth, Wellington: 1937) hereafter Stewart, *Bell*, p 115.

8. Stewart, *Bell*, p 114. For the actual wording of the telegram, see I C McGibbon, *Blue-Water Rationale: The Naval Defence of New Zealand 1914–1942* (Government Printer, Wellington: 1981) hereafter *Blue-Water Rationale*, p 24.

9. M Bassett, *Three Party Politics in New Zealand 1911–1931* (Historical Publications, Auckland: 1982) p 20.

10. *Poverty Bay Herald*, 7 November 1916, p 3.

11. *Poverty Bay Herald*, 18 December 1916, p 3.

12. *Poverty Bay Herald*, 6 November 1916, p 3.

13. *Poverty Bay Herald*, 16 January 1917, p 8. Ward had flown in May 1913 at Hendon while Leader of the Opposition. Bassett, *Ward*, pp 217–18.

14. Imperial War Conference 1917, *Minutes of Proceedings and Papers Laid before the Conference (Other Than Those Published in [Cd. 8566])*, G 40/2, NZNA, p 6.

15. Imperial War Conference 1918, *Minutes and Papers (Other than those published in [cd 9177]*, NZNA G 40/2, p 85.

16. B Gustafson, *Labour's Path to Political Independence: The Origins and Establishment of the New Zealand Labour Party 1900–19* (Auckland University Press/

Oxford University Press, Auckland: 1980) hereafter Gustafson, *Labour's Path*, p 96.

17. Gustafson, *Labour's Path*, p 96.

18. Ibid.

19. Imperial War Conference 1918, *Minutes and Papers (Other than those published in [cd 9177]*, NZNA G 40/2, p 96.

20. Imperial War Conference 1918, *Minutes and Papers (Other than those published in [cd 9177]*, NZNA G 40/2, p 203.

21. *Poverty Bay Herald*, 23 February 1917, p 6.

22. 'Draft Minutes of Imperial War Cabinet, 26 April 1917', PM 14/11, NZNA.

23. Imperial War Conference 1918, *Extracts from Minutes of Proceedings*, NZNA G40/2, p 17.

24. *NZPD*, 178, 13 July 1917, p 378.

25. Speech to Imperial War Cabinet, 13 June 1918. Quoted in D Winter, *Haig's Command: A Reassessment* (Viking, London: 1991) pp 108–09.

26. *NZPD*, 180, 13 September 1917, p 135.

27. *NZPD*, 179, 30 August 1917, p 781.

28. Imperial War Conference 1918, *Minutes and Papers (Other than those published in [cd 9177]*, NZNA G 40/2, p 175.

29. G Harper, 'Stopping the Storm: The New Zealand Division and the Kaiser's Battle (*Kaiserschlacht*) March-April 1918', in Crawford and McGibbon, *New Zealand's Great War*, pp 266–86.

30. *NZPD*, 183, 5 December 1918, p 822.

4: New Zealand's Interests

1. *NZPD*, 183, 28 November 1918, p 540.

2. *Poverty Bay Herald*, 18 February 1919, p 5.

3. *Press*, 16 December 1918, p 6.

4. *Grey River Argus*, 27 December 1916, p 8.

5. *Poverty Bay Herald*, 29 January 1917, p 3.

6. *Press*, 14 May 1919, p 6.

7. Imperial War Conference 1918, *Extracts from Minutes of Proceedings*, NZNA G40/2, p 159.

8. *Poverty Bay Herald*, 7 November 1916, p 3.

9. *NZPD*, 196, 18 August 1922, pp 484–85.

10. *NZPD*, 179, 7 August 1917, pp 31–32.

11. *NZPD*, 182, 15 April 1918, p 225.

12. *NZPD*, 183, 28 November 1918, p 539.

13. *NZPD*, 183, 5 December 1918, p 822.

14. *Poverty Bay Herald*, 22 January 1919, p 3.

15. *NZPD*, 178, 3 July 1917, p 67.

16. Ibid., p 68.

17. *New Zealand Herald*, 25 November 1918, p 4.

18. *NZPD*, 178, 27 July 1917, p 790.

19. Kay, 'In Pursuit of Victory', pp.153–54. See also *Poverty Bay Herald*, 3 February 1917, p 3, which quotes Massey and Ward as saying, 'New Zealand will never give up Samoa'.

20. This is a guarded reference to a proposal which Massey strongly supported; that much, if not all, of French Polynesia might be swapped for ceding complete control over the New Hebrides to Paris. 'Minutes of the Sub-Committee of the Imperial War Cabinet on Territorial Desiderata in the Terms of Peace, 17 April 1917', PM 14/34, NZNA.

21. *NZPD*, 183, p 1117.

22. *New Zealand Herald*, 14 December 1918, p 8.

23. *NZPD*, 181, 19 October 1917, p 278. In April Massey had raised the possibility of buying American Samoa in the Imperial War Cabinet. 'Minutes of the Sub-Committee of the Imperial War Cabinet on Territorial Desiderata in the Terms of Peace, 17 April 1917', PM 14/34, NZNA.

24. *Poverty Bay Herald*, 25 June 1919, p 6.

25. Both Massey and Ward insisted in Parliament that Germany should surrender unconditionally. *NZPD*, 183, 25 October 1918, p 8.

26. Imperial War Conference 1918, *Minutes and Papers (Other than those published in [cd 9177]*, NZNA G 40/2, pp 34–37.

27. *NZPD*, 183, 28 November 1918, p 538.

28. *NZPD*, 178, 27 July 1917, p 791.

29. *NZPD*, 181, 19 October 1917, p 276.

30. *Press*, 18 March 1919, p 6.

31. *New Zealand Herald*, 4 February 1919, p 4.

32. *Otago Daily Times*, 24 January 1919, p 4.

33. Allen to Massey, 21 January 1919, p 11–12, J. Allen Papers, Box 9, Miscellaneous Papers 1916–19, NZNA.

34. Allen to Massey, 21 January 1919, p 11–12, J. Allen Papers, Box 9, Miscellaneous Papers 1916–19, NZNA.

35. *NZPD*, 183, 5 December 1918, p 822. Four days later he declared New Zealand's interest *if anything in the way of indemnities were to be obtained from Germany*. *NZPD*, 183, 9 December 1918, p 950.

36. *NZPD*, 183, 28 November 1918, p 539.

37. *New Zealand Herald*, 7 December 1918, p 8.

38. *Press*, 30 November 1918, p 8.

39. *NZPD*, 183, p 1073.

40. *NZPD*, 183, 1 November 1918, p 170.

41. *NZPD*, 183, 28 November 1918, p 539.

42. *Poverty Bay Herald*, 11 September 1920, pp 2–3.

43. Imperial Conference 1921, *Notes of Meetings (Nos. E1 to E84)*, (HM Stationery Office, London E6: 1921) p 15.

44. *Poverty Bay Herald*, 15 April 1919, p 3.

5: Negotiations

1. In 1906 New Zealand had been represented by Joseph Ward at the International Postal Congress. Bassett, *Sir Joseph Ward*, pp 138–40.

2. *NZPD*, 191, 19 October 1921, p 643.

3. Massey to Allen, 13 February 1919, J. Allen Papers, Box 9, Miscellaneous Papers 1916–19, NZNA.

4. Massey to Allen, 26 April 1919, J. Allen Papers, Box 9, Miscellaneous Papers 1916–19, NZNA.

5. United States Department of State, *Papers Relating to the Foreign Relations of the United States: The Paris Peace Conference, 1919* (US Government Printing Office, Washington: 1943) Vol 3, pp 531–32, herafter *FRUS*. Wilson was particularly concerned about the feelings of Latin American nations, especially Brazil (hardly in any sense a 'smaller state'), which had been exposed to considerable German influence before the war. He got three representatives for Brazil.

6. *FRUS*, Vol 3, pp 531–32.

7. *NZPD*, 183, 6 November 1918, p 198.

8. Kay, 'In Pursuit of Victory', p 236.

9. *NZPD*, 183, 5 December 1918, p 824.

10. Allen to Massey, 21 January 1919, p 13, J. Allen Papers, Box 9, Miscellaneous Papers 1916–19, NZNA.

11. *NZPD*, 183, 9 December 1918, p 952.

12. *FRUS*, Vol 3, p 752.

13. *Grey River Argus*, 22 March 1919, p 4. It was Sir Maurice Hankey who dubbed Massey and Ward 'the Siamese Twins'.
14. *Poverty Bay Herald*, 8 August 1919, p 6.
15. *Grey River Argus*, 23 January 1919, p 3.
16. *Poverty Bay Herald*, 25 January 1919, p 3. He maintained that New Zealand's was *as much entitled to two delegates as outside countries like Siam and Hedjaz.*
17. *Poverty Bay Herald*, 24 January 1919, p 3. The *if* appears significant, given Massey's later reservations about any of the Dominions being represented separately.
18. *Press*, 29 January 1919, p.6; *Otago Daily Times*, 27 January 1919, p 4.
19. *NZ Truth*, 22 February 1919, p 1.
20. MacMillan, *Peacemakers*, p 53.
21. Quoted in *Poverty Bay Herald*, 25 June 1919, p 6.
22. MacMillan, *Peacemakers*, p 53.
23. *Poverty Bay Herald*, 20 February 1919, p 3.
24. *Poverty Bay Herald*, 23 January 1919, p.5; 27 January 1919, p 5.
25. *Grey River Argus*, 28 January 1919, p 3.
26. *Press*, 23 January 1919, p 6.
27. *Poverty Bay Herald*, 29 January 1919, p 3.
28. Allen to Massey, 30 April 1919, J. Allen Papers, Box 3, M1/49, NZNA.
29. Kay, 'In Pursuit of Victory', p 250. The devastating impact in Western Samoa of the Spanish influenza, introduced due to the Administration's negligence, appears to have particularly undermined support for New Zealand rule.

30. H J Hiery, *The Neglected War The German South Pacific and the Influence of World War I* (University of Hawai'i Press, Honolulu: 1995), p 172.
31. *FRUS*, Vol 3, p 753.
32. The *New Zealand Herald* in particular had made this comparison in an editorial Massey had probably read. *New Zealand Herald*, 23 November 1918, p 6.
33. *FRUS*, vol 3, pp 753–54.
34. Massey to Allen, 13 February 1919, J. Allen Papers, Box 9, Miscellaneous Papers 1916–19, NZNA.
35. Massey to Bell, 17 March 1919, MS-Papers-5210–102, Alexander Turnbull Library.
36. *Poverty Bay Herald*, 12 May 1919, p 3.
37. R G H Kay, 'Caging the Prussian Dragon: New Zealand and the Paris Peace Conference 1919', in Crawford and McGibbon, *New Zealand's Great War*, pp 123–4.
38. *New Zealand Herald*, 31 March 1919, p 6.
39. *Press*, 21 April 1919, p 6.
40. *NZ Truth*, 25 October 1919, p 1.
41. *Poverty Bay Herald*, 14 March 1919, p 6.
42. Kay, 'In Pursuit of Victory', pp 265–67.
43. *Poverty Bay Herald*, 23 April 1919, p 3.
44. *Poverty Bay Herald*, 2 July 1919, p 6.
45. *Poverty Bay Herald*, 10 March 1919, p 3. There seemed to be no suggestion that Allied troops should be investigated for any of these offences.
46. *Poverty Bay Herald*, 14 March 1919, p 6.
47. *Poverty Bay Herald*, 26 July 1919, p 5.
48. *Poverty Bay Herald*, 9 May 1919, p 3.
49. *Grey River Argus*, 2 June 1919, p 3.
50. *Poverty Bay Herald*, 19 June 1919, p 6.

51. Massey to Allen, 26 April 1919, J. Allen Papers, Box 9, Miscellaneous Papers 1916–19, NZNA.
52. Massey to Bell, 17 March 1919, MS-Papers-5210–102, Alexander Turnbull Library.
53. Massey to Allen, 13 February 1919, J. Allen Papers, Box 9, Miscellaneous Papers 1916–19, NZNA.
54. Massey to Allen, 26 April 1919, J. Allen Papers, Box 9, Miscellaneous Papers 1916–19, NZNA.
55. *NZPD*, 184, 2 September 1919, p 39. The signing was accompanied by stamping with a personal seal. According to Keith Murdoch, Massey unsuccessfully searched Paris for a seal with his initials on it. 'At last he discovered, in a pawnshop, a heavy ancient seal, bearing the letters "N.Z." and with this the Treaty was stamped.' *Poverty Bay Herald*, 3 July 1919, p 3. However, Massey ruined a good story by revealing that the seal with the initials of New Zealand on it had been obtained at an ordinary shop. *Poverty Bay Herald*, 11 August 1919, p 5.
56. *Poverty Bay Herald*, 30 June 1919, p 6.

6: Reactions to the Peace Treaties

1. *Poverty Bay Herald*, 13 May 1919, p 3.
2. *NZPD*, 2 September 1919, p 36.
3. *Otautau Standard and Wallace County Chronicle*, 13 May 1919, p 1.
4. *NZPD*, Vo1.204, 2 September 1919, p 71.
5. *New Zealand Herald*, 5 May 1919, p 6.
6. *New Zealand Herald*, 19 April 1919, p 6.
7. *New Zealand Herald*, 9 May 1919, p 6.
8. *Otago Daily Times*, 9 May 1919, p 4.
9. *Otago Daily Times*, 1 March 1919, p 6.

10. *Otago Daily Times*, 18 February 1919, p 4.
11. *Otago Daily Times*, 11 February 1919, p 4.
12. *Press*, 12 May 1919, p 6.
13. *Press*, 13 March 1919, p 6.
14. *Press*, 9 June 1919, p 6.
15. *Maoriland Worker*, 16 July 1919, p 2.
16. *NZ Truth*, 16 July 1921, p 1. The pen with which Massey signed the Treaty, together with the seal that had to be bought in Paris at short notice, is held in the collection of historic memorabilia in the House of Representatives in Wellington. It was recently part of a display celebrating New Zealand's signing of the Treaty of Versailles.

7: New Zealand and the World, 1919–25

1. *NZPD*, 191, 4 October 1921, p 184.
2. *NZPD*, 200, 26 June 1923, p 292.
3. *NZPD*, 193, 18 January 1922, p 428.
4. *NZPD*, 194, 10 February 1922, p 443.
5. *NZPD*, 200, 5 July 1923, p 732.
6. *Otautau Standard and Wallace County Chronicle*, 6 June 1922, p 3.
7. *Ashburton Guardian*, 2 June 1921, p 4.
8. *NZPD*, 191, 13 October 1921, p 497.
9. McGibbon, *Blue-Water Rationale*, pp 88–92.
10. *NZPD*, 191, 13 October 1921, p 510.
11. Imperial Conference 1921, *Notes of Meetings (Nos. E1 to E84)*, (HM Stationery Office, London E6: 1921) p 11.
12. *NZPD*, 191, 19 October 1921, p 643. He largely repeated this speech following the Washington Conference. *NZPD*, 196, 18 August 1922, p 481.

13. Imperial Conference 1921, *Summary of Proceedings and Documents*, (HM Stationery Office, London: 1921) p 27.
14. Imperial Conference 1921, *Summary of Proceedings and Documents*, (HM Stationery Office, London: 1921) p 28.
15. Imperial Conference 1921, *Notes of Meetings (Nos. E1 to E84)*, (HM Stationery Office, London E22: 1921) p 16–17.
16. *Minutes of Imperial Conference, 1921*, Vol I, E6, Box 2, G 40, p 16, NZNA.
17. *NZPD*, 191, 13 October 1921, p 510.
18. *NZPD*, 192, 24 November 1921, p 588.
19. *NZPD*, 193, 24 January 1922, p 649.
20. *NZPD*, 196, 18 August 1922, p 480.
21. *NZPD*, 196, 18 August 1922, p 484.
22. Imperial Conference 1921, *Minutes*, Vol I, E6, G 40/2, NZNA, p 13.
23. *NZPD*, 185, 23 October 1918, p 831.
24. Coded telegram sent via Lord Jellicoe, 11 November 1921, Lloyd George Papers, F/10/42.
25. *NZPD*, 185, 23 October 1918, p 831.
26. 'Position of British Indians in the Dominions', 15/7/21, Minutes of Meetings of Sub-Committees, Imperial Conference 1921, EA 11/8, Archives New Zealand, p 13.
27. Imperial Conference 1921, *Minutes*, Vol I, E4, G 40/2, Archives New Zealand, p 14,
28. *Evening Post* (Wellington), 30 November 1923.
29. For an exploration of Massey's attitudes to the conflict in Ireland and partition, see J Watson, '"I Am Irish Myself": W.F. Massey and Ireland, 1912–25', in Patterson, *Ulster–New Zealand Migration*, pp 255–62.
30. *NZPD*, 197, 19 September 1922, pp 79–80.
31. *NZPD*, 200, 5 July 1923, p 731.

32. Allen to Massey, 26 April 1919, p 15, J. Allen Papers, Box 9, Miscellaneous Papers 1916–19, NZNA.
33. M J Field, *Mau: Samoa's Struggle against New Zealand Oppression* (A H and A W Reed, Wellington: 1984) pp 52–71.
34. *NZPD*, 200, 26 June 1923, pp 298–99.
35. *NZPD*, 194, 10 February 1922, p 442.
36. Imperial Conference 1921, *Minutes of Meetings of Sub-Committees*, Vol 2, E(SC) p 14.
37. *NZPD*, 205, 15 October 1924, p 461.
38. *Dominion*, 6 February, 1930, p 9.

8: Domestic Politics, 1919–25

1. Speech at Papakura, *Poverty Bay Herald*, 24 November 1919, p 6. IWW was the acronym for the American revolutionary syndicalist movement, Industrial Workers of the World.
2. Ibid.
3. *Poverty Bay Herald*, 5 December 1919, p 9.
4. *NZ Truth*, 22 February 1919, p 1.
5. W J Gardner, 'W.F. Massey in Power, 1912–1925', *Political Science* (1961) p26.
6. Quoted by R M Burdon, *The New Dominion* (A.H. and A.W. Reed, Wellington: 1965) p 65.
7. Stewart, *Bell*, p 231.
8. *NZPD*, 200, 29 June 1923, p 476.
9. Stewart, *Bell*, p 231.

9: Legacy

1. *NZPD*, Vol. ,2 September 1919, p 36.
2. CAB 32/128, TNA.
3. *Otautau Standard and Wallace County Chronicle*, 13 May 1919, p 3.

Chronology

YEAR	AGE	THE LIFE AND THE LAND
1856		26 March: William Ferguson Massey born at Limavady, Co. Londonderry.
1860	4	October: NZ Wars start in Taranaki.
1862	6	October: John and Mary (William's parents) emigrate to NZ.
1870	14	December: Massey joins parents in New Zealand. First documented rugby football game played in NZ, at Nelson.
1877	21	Massey purchases threshing mill and leases small farm at Mangere.
1879	23	Universal manhood suffrage established in NZ.
1882	26	April: Massey marries Christina Paul. First shipment of refrigerated produce from NZ to Britain.
1883	27	Son (Walter William Massey) born.
1884	28	Daughter (Elizabeth Barnett) born. 22 July: NZ election won by Robert Stout and many Liberals.
1885	29	Son (John Norman) born.

YEAR	HISTORY	CULTURE
1856	Treaty of Paris ends Crimean War.	Richard Wagner begins composition of *Tristan und Isolde.*
1860	Italy united under Piedmont.	First British Open Golf Tournament.
1862	US Civil War sees first battle between two ironclad warships.	Victor Hugo, *Les Miserables.*
1870	Franco-Prussian War breaks out.	Charles Dickens dies.
1877	National Liberal Federation formed in Britain to be centralised party organisation.	Thomas Edison patents phonograph.
1879	Anglo-Zulu War begins.	James A. Bland, *Oh, Dem Golden Slippers.*
1882	Triple Alliance formed between Germany, Austria-Hungary, Italy.	Gilbert and Sullivan, *Iolanthe.* Richard Wagner, *Parsifal.*
1883	Krakatoa erupts.	Robert Louis Stevenson, *Treasure Island.*
1884	Fabian Society formed in Britain.	Mark Twain (Samuel Clemens), *The Adventures of Huckleberry Finn.*
1885	Indian National Congress formed.	Emile Zola, *Germinal.*

YEAR	AGE	THE LIFE AND THE LAND
1887	31	Son (Frank George) born. 26 September: Stout Government defeated in general election.
1889	33	Daughter (Christina 'Lottie') born. End of plural voting in NZ; electors can vote in only one constituency.
1890	34	Massey becomes President of Mangere Farmers' Club. Massey becomes a Freemason . August: Maritime Strike in NZ. 5 December: Liberals win election under John Ballance.
1891	35	January: Liberal Government takes power. Massey becomes President of Auckland Agricultural and Pastoral Society; Vice-President of opposition National Association.
1892	36	June: Colonial Office rules Governor of NZ must take advice of his Ministers. NZ Rugby Football Association formed
1893	37	Daughter (Marian Isabel) born. 27 April: Ballance dies. 1 May: Richard John Seddon becomes Premier (initially in caretaker role). 19 September: NZ women gain vote. 28 November: Liberals win landslide victory; Massey narrowly defeated for Franklin electorate.
1894	38	Christina 'Lottie' Massey dies. 9 April: Massey wins Waitemata by-election. August: Industrial Conciliation and Arbitration Act introduces compulsory arbitration in industrial disputes. October: Government Advances to Settlers Act.

YEAR	HISTORY	CULTURE
1887	Haymarket Riot in US.	Thomas Hardy, *The Woodlanders*. Gottlieb Daimler and Karl Benz exhibit first automobile.
1889	Dockers' Strike in London; Women's Franchise League formed in Britain.	Gilbert and Sullivan, *The Gondoliers*. Jerome K. Jerome, *Three Men in a Boat*.
1890	Forth Bridge opened. Massacre at Wounded Knee in US. Higher US tariffs introduced under McKinley Act.	Vincent van Gogh commits suicide. Antonín Dvořák, *Requiem*. Yorkshire wins inaugural official County Cricket Championship.
1891	Pope Leo XIII issues encyclical *Rerum Novarum*. Franco-Russian Alliance.	Paul Gauguin, *Two Tahitian Women on the Beach*. George Gissing, *New Grub Street*.
1892	General Electric Company established.	Sir Arthur Conan Doyle, *The Adventures of Sherlock Holmes*.
1893	Independent Labour Party formed in Bradford. Gandhi begins to use civil disobedience. Gladstone's second Home Rule Bill defeated.	Jean Sibelius, *Karelia Suite*. Robert Blatchford, *Merrie England*. Edvard Munch, *The Scream*.
1894	First Sino-Japanese War.	George Bernard Shaw, *Arms and the Man*.

YEAR	AGE	THE LIFE AND THE LAND
1896	40	June: Massey made Chief Opposition Whip. 4 December: Liberals under Seddon returned with substantial majority; Massey wins Franklin.
1898	42	November: Old Age Pensions.
1899	43	6 December: Liberals under Seddon win another large majority at general election; Massey returned for Franklin with increased majority. Seddon pledges volunteer units to Boer War.
1900	44	Son (Allan) born, dies after five days.
1901	45	11 June: NZ takes over administration of Cook Islands.
1902	46	25 November: Massey returned for Franklin with large majority; Liberals again win general election overwhelmingly.

YEAR	HISTORY	CULTURE
1896	Italian forces defeated by Ethiopians at Adowa.	First motion pictures shown in Paris. First Olympic Games of modern era held in Athens.
1898	Spanish-American War.	Henry James, *The Turn of the Screw.*
1899	Samoan Islands divided between Germany and US. German company to build 'Berlin to Baghdad Railway'. Boer War breaks out.	Claude Monet, *Bridge over a Pond of Water Lilies.*
1900	Boxer Uprising in China. Labour Representation Committee formed Britain. Australian Commonwealth formed. Second German Naval Law passed, further developing German High Seas Fleet.	Sigmund Freud, *Interpretation of Dreams.* Edward Elgar, *The Dream of Gerontius.* First box brownie camera produced.
1901	Queen Victoria dies.	Guglielmo Marconi sends radio signal across Atlantic. Rudyard Kipling, *Kim.*
1902	Boer War ends. Anglo-Japanese Alliance signed.	James Barrie, *The Admirable Crichton.* Arthur Conan Doyle, *The Hound of the Baskervilles.*

YEAR	AGE	THE LIFE AND THE LAND
1903	47	10 September: Massey becomes Leader of Opposition.
1905	49	6 December: Massey fights first election as Leader. First official tour of Britain by NZ team, dubbed 'All Blacks' during tour.
1906	50	October: Government Advances to Workers.
1907	51	18 September: NZ becomes Dominion. 28 January–26 June: Ward overseas at Colonial Conference.
1908	52	9–15 August: American 'Great White Fleet' visits Auckland. 17 and 24 November, 1 December: Massey and Opposition make some gains in general election (held under Second Ballot system).

YEAR	HISTORY	CULTURE
1903	Women's Social and Political Union formed in Britain, campaigns for votes for women. Joseph Chamberlain launches campaign for imperial preference in Britain. Bolsheviks and Mensheviks split at Congress of Russian Social Democrat Party in London. Orville and Wilbur Wright make first controlled flight.	First feature film, *The Great Train Robbery*, Edwin Porter. Henry James, *The Ambassadors*. Pablo Picasso settles in Paris.
1905	Russo-Japanese War ends. Industrial Workers of the World (IWW) founded in Chicago. First Moroccan crisis, centred on Kaiser Wilhelm's visit to Tangier following secret agreements between France, Britain and Spain for partition of Morocco.	Albert Einstein formulates his Theory of Relativity.
1906	Liberals win landslide victory in Britain.	Beatrix Potter, *The Tale of Jeremy Fisher*.
1907	Anglo-Russian Entente.	Joseph Conrad [Korzeniowski], *The Secret Agent*.
1908	Old age pensions introduced in Britain. Austria-Hungary annexes Bosnia, increasing hostility of Serbia and Russia.	Georges Sorel, *Reflexions sur la Violence*. Kenneth Grahame, *Wind in the Willows*. Model T Ford launched.

YEAR	AGE	THE LIFE AND THE LAND
1909	53	Massey shaves off beard. 12 February; Massey adopts name Reform Party for Opposition. 20 March: NZ Government offers to pay cost of constructing dreadnought for Royal Navy. 18 June-30 September: Ward overseas at Imperial Naval Conference; sharp fall in prices for NZ's primary exports. December: NZ Defence Act passed – compulsory military training.
1911	55	6 March-25 August: Sir Joseph Ward overseas, attending Imperial Conference in London. 21 June: Ward accepts baronetcy. 5 November: John Massey dies. 7 and 14 December: Massey and Reform Party win largest number of seats in general election.
1912	56	14 May – 12 November: Industrial dispute at Waihi gold mine. 6 July: Massey and Reform defeat Liberal Government on no-confidence motion.
1913	57	21 October: major strike begins; Massey Government enrols special constables, deploys them in ports.

YEAR	HISTORY	CULTURE
1909	British Chancellor of Exchequer Lloyd George introduces 'People's Budget'. Louis Bleriot flies across Channel.	John Galsworthy, *Strife.* Gustav Mahler, *Das Lied von der Erde.*
1911	Parliament Act limits powers of House of Lords in Britain. Manchu Dynasty overthrown in China; Republic declared. Winston Churchill becomes First Lord of Admiralty. Second Moroccan crisis between Germany and Franco-British Entente, centred on despatch of German gunboat to Agadir.	Thomas Mann, *Felix Krull.* Irving Berlin, *Alexander's Ragtime Band.*
1912	Sir Edward Carson organises Ulster Volunteers. *Titanic* sinks. First Balkan War launched by Bulgaria, Serbia, Greece and Montenegro against Turkey. Irish Home Rule Bill introduced by Liberal government in Britain. Woodrow Wilson elected US President.	Georges Braque, *Le Portugais.* Jack Judge and Harry H Williams, *It's A Long Way To Tipperary.*
1913	First Balkan War ends: Turkish lose territory to opponents, Albania created. Bulgaria launches Second Balkan War; defeated by Serbia, Greece, Romania and Turkey; loses considerable territory.	Filippo Marinetti, *Le Futurisme.* Alfred North Whitehead and Bertrand Russell, *Principia Mathematica.*

YEAR	AGE	THE LIFE AND THE LAND
1914	58	5 August: Massey joins with Ward as Governor Lord Liverpool reads proclamation of war with Germany. 29 August: NZ Expeditionary Force seizes Western Samoa from Germans. 16 October: Main Body of NZEF leaves for Egypt. 10 December: Massey and Reform win very narrow victory in general election.
1915	59	25 April: ANZAC landings at Gallipoli. April: Frank George Massey volunteers. 4 August: Massey forms Coalition Government with Liberals under Ward. 18–20 December: Withdrawal from Gallipoli.

YEAR	HISTORY	CULTURE
1914	World War I: Archduke Franz Ferdinand assassinated in Sarajevo; Austria-Hungary declares war on Serbia; Germany, Austria-Hungary declare war on Russia, France; Britain enters war following German invasion of Belgium; Japan enters war on Allied side; Russians defeated at Tannenberg and the Masurian Lakes; German advance halted at Battle of the Marne; Turkey enters war on Germany's side; Von Spee's East Asiatic Squadron destroys British squadron off Coronel in Chile, destroyed off Falkland Islands. Panama Canal opens. W M Hughes becomes Labor Prime Minister of Australia.	Paul Peguy killed in action. Edgar Rice Burroughs, *Tarzan of the Apes*.
1915	Unsuccessful naval attack on Dardanelles. *Lusitania* sunk. First Zeppelin raid on London. Italy enters war on Allied side. Bulgaria enters war on German side. Allied forces land at Salonika. Nurse Edith Cavell executed. Sir Douglas Haig becomes commander of British forces on Western Front.	Rupert Brooke, *The Soldier*, dies during Dardanelles Campaign. Rudyard Kipling's son Jack killed in action. First showing of *Birth of a Nation* by D W Griffiths.

YEAR	AGE	THE LIFE AND THE LAND
1916	60	7–8 July: NZ Labour Party formed around opposition to conscription.
		1 August: Conscription introduced under Military Service Act.
		August: Massey and Ward leave for London; attend Imperial War Conference.
		September: NZD fights in later stages of Battle of the Somme.
		November: Massey visits Limavady.
1917	61	June: Massey and Ward return from Imperial War Conference/ Imperial War Cabinet.
		7 June: NZD fights at Battle of Messines.
		October: NZD suffers heavy casualties at Battle of Passchendaele
		9 December: Allied forces under General Allenby, including NZ Mounted Rifle Brigade, advance in Palestine, capturing Jerusalem.
		December: All public bars to close at 6 pm (remains in force until 1967).

YEAR	HISTORY	CULTURE
1916	Battle of Verdun. British forces surrender at Kut-el-Amara. Easter Rising in Dublin. Coalition Government formed in Britain; conscription introduced. Battle of Jutland. Hughes leaves Australian Labor Party over conscription. Wilson re-elected President with slogan 'He Kept Us Out of the War'. Lloyd George becomes Prime Minister of Britain.	James Joyce, *Portrait of the Artist as a Young Man*. John Buchan, *Greenmantle*.
1917	First Russian Revolution: Tsar abdicates. Second Russian Revolution: brings Bolsheviks to power. Italian defeat at Caporetto. Georges Clemenceau becomes Prime Minister of France. Balfour Declaration: support for 'Jewish national home' in Palestine provided 'rights of non-Jewish communities' there safeguarded.	Jerome Kern and P G Wodehouse, *Oh, Boy*. Edgar Leslie, E Ray Goetz and George W Meyer, *For Me and My Gal*. George M Cohan, *Over There*. L M Montgomery, *Anne's House of Dreams*.

YEAR	AGE	THE LIFE AND THE LAND
1918	62	April: NZD helps halt German advance; joins offensive that drives them back towards the Rhine. May: Massey and Ward leave for London, attend Imperial War Cabinet. May: Frank George Massey seriously wounded. October: Allied forces, including NZ Mounted Rifle Brigade, advance through Syria. 12 October: Massey and Ward return from London. 12 December: Massey and Ward leave to attend Paris Peace Conference.

YEAR	HISTORY	CULTURE
1918	Wilson sets out Fourteen Points. Treaty of Brest-Litovsk: Russia withdraws from war, massive territorial loss, huge indemnity. US enters war. Treaty of Bucharest: Romania withdraws from war, massive territorial loss, huge indemnity. German Spring Offensive brings significant Allied losses. Allies halt German offensive, drive German armies back. Bulgaria, Turkey, Austria-Hungary agree armistices. Kaiser Wilhelm II abdicates. Germany granted armistice. Women over 30 granted vote/ right to be elected to Parliament in Britain. Lloyd George/ Coalition win British general election.	Marie Stopes, *Married Love*. Wilfred Owen killed in action. Lytton Strachey, *Eminent Victorians*.

YEAR	AGE	THE LIFE AND THE LAND
1919	63	22 January: Massey becomes NZ Delegate at Paris Peace Conference.
		30 January: Clash with President Wilson over mandatory system.
		February-March: Massey secures agreement NZ to have mandate for Western Samoa.
		26 March: Massey supports Hughes in opposition to Japanese proposal for racial equality clause in League of Nations Covenant.
		10 April: Prohibition narrowly defeated in referendum.
		11 April: Wilson rules against inclusion of racial equality clause despite majority support.
		11 April Massey forced to accept Inter-Allied Reparations Commission would decide amount of reparations.
		7 May: Massey and Ward attend presentation of draft peace treaty to German delegates.
		7 May: allocation of mandates with Western Samoa to NZ, Nauru to Britain.
		28 June: Massey signs Treaty of Versailles.
		2 July: Agreement between Australia, NZ and Britain on distribution of Nauru phosphate.
		5 August: Massey and Ward return to NZ.
		21 August: Ward announces end of Coalition Government. NZ Women given right to be elected to Parliament.
		17 December: Massey and Reform win comfortable victory with low share of vote in turbulent general election; Prohibition very narrowly defeated.
1920	64	Lord Jellicoe becomes Governor-General of NZ.
		November: Immigration Restriction Amendment Act; Marriage Amendment Act.
		December: League of Nations officially assigns Western Samoa to NZ as 'C' mandate.

YEAR	HISTORY	CULTURE
1919	Spartacists suppressed in Berlin. Paris Peace Conference opens. Weimar Republic established. Soviet Government established in Budapest under Bela Kun. Bolsheviks form Third International (Comintern). 379 Indians killed in Amritsar Massacre. Treaty of Trianon signed with Hungary. Treaty of Versailles signed with Germany. Treaty of St Germain signed with Austria. Treaty of Neuilly signed with Bulgaria.	Siegfried Sassoon, *War Poems.* John Maynard Keynes, *The Economic Consequences of the Peace.*
1920	Prohibition introduced in US. Russian anti-Communist forces defeated. Paris Peace Conference closes. Treaty of Sèvres signed with Turkey. Government of Ireland Act initiates partition. Warren G Harding elected US President	Katherine Mansfield, *Bliss and Other Stories.* Edith Wharton, *The Age of Innocence.*

YEAR	AGE	THE LIFE AND THE LAND
1921	65	NZ Communist Party formed. Large fall in prices for NZ's primary exports. May–September: Massey travels overseas, attends Imperial Conference.
1922	66	February: Meat Export Control Act passed; Board controlled by producers to supervise meat exports established. May: Bishop Liston tried for sedition. September: Massey Government calls for volunteers for possible war with Turkey during Chanak crisis. 7 December: Massey and Reform Party lose majority in election, forced to depend on Liberals opposed to Liberal Government dependent on Labour Party.
1923	67	June: Maui Pomare becomes NZ Minister of Health August: Dairy Produce Export Control Act passed, Board controlled by producers to supervise dairy exports established. 28 August: Massey travels overseas, attends Imperial Conference, Imperial Economic Conference. November–December: Massey supports Conservative Party in British general election on issue of imperial preference.
1924	68	January: Massey returns to NZ November: Massey becomes NZ Freemasons Grand Master.

YEAR	HISTORY	CULTURE
1921	Anglo-Irish Treaty signed. Parliament of Northern Ireland opened.	*The Kid*, starring Charlie Chaplin. D H Lawrence, *Women in Love*.
1922	Washington Conference: ends Anglo-Japanese Alliance, agrees ratios for capital ships between major powers. Treaty of Rapallo signed between Germany and Soviet Union. 'March on Rome' brings Mussolini to power. Lloyd George replaced by Bonar Law as Prime Minister of Britain.	British Broadcasting Company established. Howard Carter discovers Tutankhamen's tomb. T S Eliot, *The Wasteland*. George Orwell [Eric Blair] joins Indian Imperial Police in Burma.
1923	French and Belgian troops occupy Ruhr to enforce reparation payments. Hughes resigns as Australian Prime Minister. Treaty of Lausanne with Turkey. Italy briefly occupies Corfu. Hitler's attempted 'Beer Hall Putsch' in Munich.	Katherine Mansfield dies. L Frank Baum, *The Cowardly Lion of Oz*.
1924	Lenin dies. Minority Labour Government comes to power in Britain. Dawes Plan drawn up to recalculate German reparations. Construction of Singapore Naval Base halted. Labour Government in Britain defeated in general election.	*The Thief of Baghdad,* starring Douglas Fairbanks. British Empire Exhibition at Wembley. E.M. Forster, *A Passage to India*.

YEAR	AGE	THE LIFE AND THE LAND
1925	69	10 May: Massey dies.

YEAR	HISTORY	CULTURE
1925	United Kingdom returns to gold standard. Treaties of Locarno signed.	Theodore Dreiser, *An American Tragedy*. Franz Kafka's *The Trial* published posthumously.

Bibliographical Note

Unlike many of the other participants in the Paris Peace Conference, William Massey has had relatively little written about him and he never seems to have been tempted to write his memoirs or even his recollections of the Conference. In 2008 an independent scholar, Bruce Farland, published a substantial biography of the man, entitled *Farmer Bill*. This work is focused very much on his political career in New Zealand and takes to task many of Massey's contemporary and later critics. Otago University Press is also looking to publish a collection of essays by New Zealand historians revisiting Massey's reputation in a range of areas. These essays generally arise from papers presented at the massey@massey conference in 2006. The works of W J Gardner, while dating from four decades ago, remain very fruitful sources of ideas on Massey, both as political aspirant and Prime Minister. During the same period, the University of Auckland historian Peter O'Connor directed a lot of attention to what he saw as Massey's shortcomings as a 'bigoted' Orangeman and Machiavellian manipulator of New Zealand's politics. Miles Fairburn was responsible for launching the current reappraisal of Massey and his role. The most accessible of Fairburn's articles in that regard is probably 'The Farmers Take Over (1912–1930)', in Keith Sinclair (ed), *The Oxford Illustrated History of New Zealand*. For an appreciation of how Fairburn's approach relates to the wider social and cultural development of New Zealand, see his 'The Rural Myth and the New Urban Frontier: An Approach to New Zealand Social History', published in the *New Zealand Journal of History* in 1975, and 'Why Did the New Zealand Labour Party Fail to Win Office until 1935?', published in *Political Science* in 1985.

Some of the more inveterate of Massey's domestic opponents are captured in Erik Olssen's work *The Red Feds: Revolutionary Industrial Unionism and the New Zealand Federation of Labour 1908–14*. For a fascinating examination of part of urban New Zealand during this period, see the same author's *Building the New World: Work, Politics and Society in Caversham 1880s-1920s*.

None of these works has much to say on Massey at the Paris Peace Conference. The historian of New Zealand at that event, and indeed of Anglo-New Zealand relations during the First World War, is Richard Kay. That whole area was examined in his University of Otago doctoral thesis, 'In Pursuit of Victory: British-New Zealand Relations during the First World War'. Dr Kay has examined Massey's performance at the Peace Conference itself in a published article, 'Caging the Prussian Dragon: New Zealand and the Paris Peace Conference 1919', in John Crawford and Ian McGibbon (eds), *New Zealand's Great War: New Zealand, the Allies and the First World War*.

Many general histories of New Zealand have been published and continue to be published. However, for an appreciation of at least some of the complexities of the country's history, I would recommend reading *The Oxford History of*

New Zealand, second edition, edited by Geoffrey W Rice. For an overview by a single author, see the two volumes by James Belich, *Making Peoples: A History of the New Zealanders from Polynesian Settlement to the End of the Nineteenth Century* and *Paradise Reforged: A History of the New Zealanders from the 1880s to the Year 2000*. In *Replenishing the Earth: The Settler Revolution and the Rise of the Anglo-world, 1783–1939*, Belich has recently placed New Zealand in a global context that certainly resonates in the experience of Bill Massey.

Readers will find that many of the Notes to this work refer to comparatively obscure provincial newspapers in New Zealand, such as the *Poverty Bay Herald*, the *Ashburton Guardian* and the *Grey River Argus*. This is because the National Library in Wellington has made much of the text of a substantial number of such newspapers available online as part of a project entitled 'Papers Past'. Not only does this make the material readily accessible to researchers, but it also means that readers of their work throughout the world can look up the original references. Unfortunately the Library has not been able to digitise most of the major newspapers in the main centres of New Zealand in this way, so those publications have to be accessed through microfilm or hard copy, generally within New Zealand itself. As the provincial newspapers received and published the same material from the wire services as their main-centre counterparts, and indeed sometimes reprinted the latter's own stories, they are vastly more useful for research on topics of national importance than their places of publication might suggest.

Bibliography

Published official documents

Appendices to the Journals of the House of Representatives (New Zealand)

New Zealand Parliamentary Debates

New Zealand Statutes

United States Department of State, *Papers Relating to the Foreign Relations of the United States: The Paris Peace Conference, 1919* (US Government Printing Office, 1943)

Biographies and memoirs

M Bassett, *Sir Joseph Ward: A Political Biography* (Auckland University Press, 1993)

H J Constable, *From Ploughboy to Premier* (John Marlowe Savage and Co., 1925)

W J Gardner, *William Massey*, (A H and A W Reed, 1969)

B Farland, *Farmer Bill: William Ferguson Massey and the Reform Party* (Bruce Farland, 2008)

D Lloyd George, *The Truth about the Peace Treaties*, 2 vols (Victor Gollancz, 1938)

G H Scholefield, *The Right Honourable William Ferguson Massey, M.P., P.C., Prime Minister of New Zealand, 1912–1925: A Personal Biography* (Tombs, 1925)

W D Stewart, *The Right Honourable Sir Francis H.D. Bell, P.C., G.C.M.G., K.C., His Life and Times* (Butterworth, 1937)

Secondary sources

P Baker, *King and Country Call: New Zealanders, Conscription and the Great War* (Auckland University Press, 1988)

M Bassett, *Sir Joseph Ward: A Political Biography* (Auckland University Press, 1993)

M Bassett, *Three Party Politics in New Zealand 1911–1931* (Historical Publications, 1982)

J Belich, *Making Peoples: A History of the New Zealanders from Polynesian Settlement to the End of the Nineteenth Century* (Allen Lane/Penguin, 1996)

J Belich, *Paradise Reforged: A History of the New Zealanders from the 1880s to the Year 2000* (Allen Lane/ Penguin, 2001)

J Belich, *Replenishing the Earth: The Settler Revolution and the Rise of the Anglo-World, 1783–1939* (Oxford University Press, 2009)

R M Burdon, *The New Dominion: A Social and Political History of New Zealand 1918–39* (A H and A W Reed, 1965)

H J Constable, *From Ploughboy to Premier* (John Marlowe Savage and Co., 1925)

J Crawford and I C McGibbon (Eds), *New Zealand's Great War: New Zealand, the Allies and the First World War* (Exisle Publishing, 2007)

M Fairburn, 'The Farmers Take Over (1912–1930)', in Keith Sinclair (ed), *The Oxford Illustrated History of New Zealand* (Oxford University Press, 1990) pp 185–209

M Fairburn, 'The Rural Myth and the New Urban Frontier: An Approach to New Zealand Social History', *New Zealand Journal of History*, 9:1 (1975) pp 3–21.

M Fairburn, 'Why Did the New Zealand Labour Party Fail to Win Office until 1935?', *Political Science*, 37:2 (1985) pp 101–24

M J Field, *Mau: Samoa's Struggle against New Zealand Oppression* (A H and A W Reed, 1984)

W J Gardner, 'The Rise of W.F. Massey, 1891–1912', *Political Science*, 13:1 (1961) pp 3–30

W J Gardner, 'W.F. Massey in Power, 1912–1925', *Political Science*, 13:2 (1961) pp 3–30.

W J Gardner, *William Massey* (A H and A W Reed, 1969)

H George, *Progress and Poverty: An Inquiry into the Cause of Industrial Depressions and of Increase of Want with Increase of Wealth [and] the Remedy* (Kegan Paul, 1922)

B Gustafson, *Labour's Path to Political Independence: The Origins and Establishment of the New Zealand Labour Party 1900–19* (Auckland University Press, 1980)

D Hamer, *The New Zealand Liberals: The Years of Power, 1891–1912* (Auckland University Press, 1988)

G Harper, *Massacre at Passchendaele:The New Zealand Story* (HarperCollins Publishers, 2000)

G Harper, *Spring offensive: New Zealand and the second Battle of the Somme* (HarperCollins Publishers, 2003)

G Harper, *Dark Journey*, (HarperCollins Publishers, 2007)

H J Hiery, *The Neglected War: The German South Pacific and the Influence of World War I* (University of Hawai'i Press, 1995)

R G H Kay, 'Caging the Prussian Dragon: New Zealand and the Paris Peace Conference 1919', in John Crawford and Ian McGibbon (eds), *New Zealand's Great War: New Zealand, the Allies and the First World War* (Exisle Publishing, 2007)

R G H Kay, 'In Pursuit of Victory: British-New Zealand Relations during the First World War' (University of Otago PhD Thesis, 2001)

M MacMillan, *Peacemakers: The Paris Conference of 1919 and Its Attempt to End War* (John Murray, 2001)

I C McGibbon, *Blue-Water Rationale: The Naval Defence of New Zealand 1914–1942* (New Zealand Government Printer, 1981)

I C McGibbon (ed), *The Oxford Companion to New Zealand Military History* (Oxford University Press, 2000)

P S O'Connor, 'Some Political Preoccupations of Mr Massey, 1918–20', *Political Science*, 18:2 (1966) pp 16–38

P S O'Connor, 'Mr Massey and the P.P.A. – a Suspicion Confirmed', *New Zealand Journal of Public Administration*, 28:2 (1966) pp 69–74

P S O'Connor, 'Sectarian Conflict in New Zealand, 1911–1920, *Political Science*, 19:1 (1967) pp3–16

W H Oliver, 'Social Policy in New Zealand: An Historical Overview', *New Zealand Today*, vol. I, *The Royal Commission on Social Policy April Report* (The Commission, 1988) pp 1–45.

E Olssen, *Building the New World: Work, Politics and Society in Caversham 1880s-1920s* (Auckland University Press, 1995)

E Olssen, *The Red Feds: Revolutionary Industrial Unionism and the New Zealand Federation of Labour 1908–14* (Oxford University Press, 1988)

B Patterson (ed), *Ulster-New Zealand Migration and Cultural Transfers* (Four Courts, 2006)

C Pugsley, *Gallipoli: The New Zealand Story* (Penguin, 2008)

G W Rice (ed), *The Oxford History of New Zealand*, second ed. (Oxford University Press, 1981)

G H Scholefield, *The Right Honourable William Ferguson Massey, M.P., P.C., Prime Minister of New Zealand, 1912–1925: A Personal Biography* (Tombs, 1925)

R Sweetman, *Bishop in the Dock: The Sedition Trial of James Liston*, (Auckland University Press, 1997)

D Winter, *Haig's Command: A Reassessment* (Viking, 1991)

Picture Sources

The author and publishers wish to express their thanks to the following sources of illustrative material and/or permission to reproduce it. They will make proper acknowledgements in future editions in the event that any omissions have occurred.

Illustrations courtesy of Topham Picturepoint.

Endpapers
The Signing of Peace in the Hall of Mirrors, Versailles, 28th June 1919 by Sir William Orpen (Imperial War Museum: Bridgeman Art Library)
Front row: Dr Johannes Bell (Germany) signing with Herr Hermann Müller leaning over him
Middle row (seated, left to right): General Tasker H Bliss, Col E M House, Mr Henry White, Mr Robert Lansing, President Woodrow Wilson (United States); M Georges Clemenceau (France); Mr David Lloyd George, Mr Andrew Bonar Law, Mr Arthur J Balfour, Viscount Milner, Mr G N Barnes (Great Britain); Prince Saionji (Japan)
Back row (left to right): M Eleftherios Venizelos (Greece);

Dr Afonso Costa (Portugal); Lord Riddell (British Press);
Sir George E Foster (Canada); M Nikola Pašić (Serbia);
M Stephen Pichon (France); Col Sir Maurice Hankey,
Mr Edwin S Montagu (Great Britain); the Maharajah of
Bikaner (India); Signor Vittorio Emanuele Orlando (Italy);
M Paul Hymans (Belgium); General Louis Botha (South
Africa); Mr W M Hughes (Australia)

Jacket images

(Front): Imperial War Museum: akg Images.
(Back): *Peace Conference at the Quai d'Orsay* by Sir William
Orpen (Imperial War Museum: akg Images).
Left to right (seated): Signor Orlando (Italy); Mr Robert
Lansing, President Woodrow Wilson (United States); M
Georges Clemenceau (France); Mr David Lloyd George, Mr
Andrew Bonar Law, Mr Arthur J Balfour (Great Britain);
Left to right (standing): M Paul Hymans (Belgium); Mr
Eleftherios Venizelos (Greece); The Emir Feisal (The
Hashemite Kingdom); Mr W F Massey (New Zealand);
General Jan Smuts (South Africa); Col E M House (United
States); General Louis Botha (South Africa); Prince Saionji
(Japan); Mr W M Hughes (Australia); Sir Robert Borden
(Canada); Mr G N Barnes (Great Britain); M Ignacy
Paderewski (Poland)

Index

empire, and *see* British
Empire
First World War, and 42,
44, 66, 101, 110–11
New Zealand, and 6,
12–13, 15, 22, 44, 48, 50,
53–4, 57, 65, 67, 74–6,
95–8, 125, 138, 151, 155
British Empire viii, 21, 28, 44,
49, 55–7, 65, 70–1, 74–6,
83–5, 90, 94, 97, 100, 109,
118, 123–6, 128–31, 135–6,
139, 143, 149–51
British Empire delegation 70,
85, 90, 94, 96, 98, 100, 102
Bulgaria ix, 59, 107
butter 12–13, 54, 57, 147

C

Canada 14, 55, 79, 86, 138,
150
Canterbury (NZ) 8, 17, 26,
70, 145
Carroll, Sir James 87–8
Catholics 6, 13, 20, 23, 25,
35–7, 52, 143, 146–7
Chamberlain, Austen 51
Chanak crisis 132, 138
cheese 12–13, 147
China 14, 125–6, 155
Christchurch 20, 22, 35, 37,
66, 78, 81, 99, 116, 144
Church Missionary Society
[CMS] 6–7
Clemenceau, Georges 72,
105
coal mining 52, 141–2

Colonial Office 14, 104
conscription 42–3, 50–2, 88
Cook islands 75, 94
Cost of Living Act 54, 57
Craig, Sir James 131, 138
Czechoslovakia 113–14

D

Defence Act (1909) 21
de Valera, Eamon 130, 147
Dominions 15, 42, 49, 55, 70,
77, 79, 82, 84–6, 89–90, 95,
97, 99, 105–6, 112, 127–8,
132–3, 139, 150–1
Dublin 49–50, 52
Dunedin 11, 43, 79, 115

E

Egypt 47, 49, 72, 126
Elliott, Reverend Howard 52,
143, 145

F

faipules [chiefs] 134
Fairburn, Miles xi, 18, 194–5
Far East 126, 155
Federation of Labour xi, 142,
195
Ferguson, Sir Ronald Munro
46
First World War xi, 22, 39, 42,
46, 70, 88, 110, 135, 150
Fourteen Points 67–9, 125
France 49, 73, 85, 106, 110,
123–5, 130, 155, 157
Fraser, Peter 114–15
freehold 24, 38–9, 83, 94

Makers
of the
Modern
World

UK PUBLICATION: November 2008 to December 2010
CLASSIFICATION: Biography/History/
     International Relations
FORMAT: 198 × 128mm
EXTENT: 208pp
ILLUSTRATIONS: 6 photographs plus 4 maps
TERRITORY: world

Chronology of life in context, full index, bibliography innovative layout
with sidebars

Woodrow Wilson: United States of America by Brian Morton
Friedrich Ebert: Germany by Harry Harmer
Georges Clemenceau: France by David Watson
David Lloyd George: Great Britain by Alan Sharp
Prince Saionji: Japan by Jonathan Clements
Wellington Koo: China by Jonathan Clements
Eleftherios Venizelos: Greece by Andrew Dalby
From the Sultan to Atatürk: Turkey by Andrew Mango
The Hashemites: The Dream of Arabia by Robert McNamara
Chaim Weizmann: The Dream of Zion by Tom Fraser
Piip, Meierovics & Voldemaras: Estonia, Latvia & Lithuania by Charlotte Alston
Ignacy Paderewski: Poland by Anita Prazmowska
Beneš, Masaryk: Czechoslovakia by Peter Neville
Károlyi & Bethlen: Hungary by Bryan Cartledge
Karl Renner: Austria by Jamie Bulloch
Vittorio Orlando: Italy by Spencer Di Scala
Pašić & Trumbić: The Kingdom of Serbs, Croats and Slovenes by Dejan Djokic
Aleksandŭr Stamboliĭski: Bulgaria by R J Crampton
Ion Bratianu: Romania by Keith Hitchin
Paul Hymans: Belgium by Sally Marks
General Smuts: South Africa by Antony Lentin
William Hughes: Australia by Carl Bridge
William Massey: New Zealand by James Watson
Sir Robert Borden: Canada by Martin Thornton
Maharajah of Bikaner: India by Hugh Purcell
Afonso Costa: Portugal by Filipe Ribeiro de Meneses
Epitácio Pessoa: Brazil by Michael Streeter
South America by Michael Streeter
Central America by Michael Streeter
South East Asia by Andrew Dalby
The League of Nations by Ruth Henig
Consequences of Peace: The Versailles Settlement – Aftermath and Legacy
     by Alan Sharp